FREEDOM
from the
KNOWN

Dear Debbie & Enol,
   Just wanted to
share my favorite Mind
with you.

          Much love,
          Point.

FREEDOM
from the
KNOWN

by
J. Krishnamurti

EDITED BY MARY LUTYENS

HarperSanFrancisco
A Division of HarperCollinsPublishers

LIBRARY OF CONGRESS CATALOG CARD NUMBER: 69-17013
ISBN: 0-06-064808-2

94 95 CWI 25 24

This book has been written at Krishnamurti's suggestion and has his approval. The words have been chosen from a number of his recent talks (in English), taped and previously unpublished, to audiences in various parts of the world. Their selection and the order in which they are presented are my responsibility.

M.L.

CONTENTS

I

Man's Search—The Tortured Mind—the Traditional Approach—The Trap of Respectability—The Human Being and the Individual—The Battle of Existence— The Basic Nature of Man—Responsibility—Truth— Self-transformation—Dissipation of Energy—Freedom from Authority

MAN HAS THROUGHOUT the ages been seeking something beyond himself, beyond material welfare— something we call truth or God or reality, a timeless state —something that cannot be disturbed by circumstances, by thought or by human corruption.

Man has always asked the question: what is it all about? Has life any meaning at all? He sees the enormous confusion of life, the brutalities, the revolts, the wars, the endless divisions of religion, ideology and nationality, and with a sense of deep abiding frustration he asks, what is one to do, what is this thing we call living, is there anything beyond it?

And not finding this nameless thing of a thousand names which he has always sought, he has cultivated faith—faith in a saviour or an ideal—and faith invariably breeds violence.

In this constant battle which we call living, we try to set a code of conduct according to the society in which we are brought up, whether it be a Communist society or a so-called free society; we accept a standard of behaviour

9

as part of our tradition as Hindus or Muslims or Christians or whatever we happen to be. We look to someone to tell us what is right or wrong behaviour, what is right or wrong thought, and in following this pattern our conduct and our thinking become mechanical, our responses automatic. We can observe this very easily in ourselves.

For centuries we have been spoon-fed by our teachers, by our authorities, by our books, our saints. We say, 'Tell me all about it—what lies beyond the hills and the mountains and the earth?' and we are satisfied with their descriptions, which means that we live on words and our life is shallow and empty. We are second-hand people. We have lived on what we have been told, either guided by our inclinations, our tendencies, or compelled to accept by circumstances and environment. We are the result of all kinds of influences and there is nothing new in us, nothing that we have discovered for ourselves; nothing original, pristine, clear.

Throughout theological history we have been assured by religious leaders that if we perform certain rituals, repeat certain prayers or mantras, conform to certain patterns, suppress our desires, control our thoughts, sublimate our passions, limit our appetites and refrain from sexual indulgence, we shall, after sufficient torture of the mind and body, find something beyond this little life. And that is what millions of so-called religious people have done through the ages, either in isolation, going off into the desert or into the mountains or a cave or wandering from village to village with a begging bowl, or, in a group, joining a monastery, forcing their minds to conform to an established pattern. But a tortured mind, a broken mind, a mind which wants to escape from all turmoil, which has denied the outer world and been made dull through discipline and conformity—such a mind, however long it seeks, will find only according to its own distortion.

So to discover whether there actually is or is not something beyond this anxious, guilty, fearful, competitive existence, it seems to me that one must have a completely different approach altogether. The traditional approach is from the periphery inwards, and through time, practice and renunciation, gradually to come upon that inner flower, that inner beauty and love—in fact to do everything to make oneself narrow, petty and shoddy; peel off little by little; take time; tomorrow will do, next life will do—and when at last one comes to the centre one finds there is nothing there, because one's mind has been made incapable, dull and insensitive.

Having observed this process, one asks oneself, is there not a different approach altogether—that is, is it not possible to explode from the centre?

The world accepts and follows the traditional approach. The primary cause of disorder in ourselves is the seeking of reality promised by another; we mechanically follow somebody who will assure us a comfortable spiritual life. It is a most extraordinary thing that although most of us are opposed to political tyranny and dictatorship, we inwardly accept the authority, the tyranny, of another to twist our minds and our way of life. So if we completely reject, not intellectually but actually, all so-called spiritual authority, all ceremonies, rituals and dogmas, it means that we stand alone and are already in conflict with society; we cease to be respectable human beings. A respectable human being cannot possibly come near to that infinite, immeasurable, reality.

You have now started by denying something absolutely

false—the traditional approach—but if you deny it as a reaction you will have created another pattern in which you will be trapped; if you tell yourself intellectually that this denial is a very good idea but do nothing about it, you cannot go any further. If you deny it, however, because you understand the stupidity and immaturity of it, if you reject it with tremendous intelligence, because you are free and not frightened, you will create a great disturbance in yourself and around you but you will step out of the trap of respectability. Then you will find that you are no longer seeking. That is the first thing to learn—not to seek. When you seek you are really only window-shopping.

The question of whether or not there is a God or truth or reality, or whatever you like to call it, can never be answered by books, by priests, philosophers or saviours. Nobody and nothing can answer the question but you yourself and that is why you must know yourself. Immaturity lies only in total ignorance of self. To understand yourself is the beginning of wisdom.

And what is yourself, the individual you? I think there is a difference between the human being and the individual. The individual is a local entity, living in a particular country, belonging to a particular culture, particular society, particular religion. The human being is not a local entity. He is everywhere. If the individual merely acts in a particular corner of the vast field of life, then his action is totally unrelated to the whole. So one has to bear in mind that we are talking of the whole not the part, because in the greater the lesser is, but in the lesser the greater is not. The individual is the little conditioned, miserable, frustrated entity, satisfied with his little gods and his little traditions, whereas a human being is concerned with the

total welfare, the total misery and total confusion of the world.

We human beings are what we have been for millions of years—colossally greedy, envious, aggressive, jealous, anxious and despairing, with occasional flashes of joy and affection. We are a strange mixture of hate, fear and gentleness; we are both violence and peace. There has been outward progress from the bullock cart to the jet plane but psychologically the individual has not changed at all, and the structure of society throughout the world has been created by individuals. The outward social structure is the result of the inward psychological structure of our human relationships, for the individual is the result of the total experience, knowledge and conduct of man. Each one of us is the storehouse of all the past. The individual is the human who is all mankind. The whole history of man is written in ourselves.

Do observe what is actually taking place within yourself and outside yourself in the competitive culture in which you live with its desire for power, position, prestige, name, success and all the rest of it—observe the achievements of which you are so proud, this whole field you call living in which there is conflict in every form of relationship, breeding hatred, antagonism, brutality and endless wars. This field, this life, is all we know, and being unable to understand the enormous battle of existence we are naturally afraid of it and find escape from it in all sorts of subtle ways. And we are frightened also of the unknown—frightened of death, frightened of what lies beyond tomorrow. So we are afraid of the known and afraid of the unknown. That is our daily life and in that there is no hope, and therefore every form of philosophy, every form of theological concept, is merely an escape from the actual reality of what is.

All outward forms of change brought about by wars, revolutions, reformations, laws and ideologies have failed completely to change the basic nature of man and therefore of society. As human beings living in this monstrously ugly world, let us ask ourselves, can this society, based on competition, brutality and fear, come to an end? Not as an intellectual conception, not as a hope, but as an actual fact, so that the mind is made fresh, new and innocent and can bring about a different world altogether? It can only happen, I think, if each one of us recognises the central fact that we, as individuals, as human beings, in whatever part of the world we happen to live or whatever culture we happen to belong to, are totally responsible for the whole state of the world.

We are each one of us responsible for every war because of the aggressiveness of our own lives, because of our nationalism, our selfishness, our gods, our prejudices, our ideals, all of which divide us. And only when we realise, not intellectually but actually, as actually as we would recognise that we are hungry or in pain, that you and I are responsible for all this existing chaos, for all the misery throughout the entire world because we have contributed to it in our daily lives and are part of this monstrous society with its wars, divisions, its ugliness, brutality and greed—only then will we act.

But what can a human being do—what can you and I do—to create a completely different society? We are asking ourselves a very serious question. Is there anything to be done at all? What *can* we do? Will somebody tell us? People *have* told us. The so-called spiritual leaders, who

are supposed to understand these things better than we do, have told us by trying to twist and mould us into a new pattern, and that hasn't led us very far; sophisticated and learned men have told us and that has led us no further. We have been told that all paths lead to truth—you have your path as a Hindu and someone else has his path as a Christian and another as a Muslim, and they all meet at the same door—which is, when you look at it, so obviously absurd. Truth has no path, and that is the beauty of truth, it is living. A dead thing has a path to it because it is static, but when you see that truth is something living, moving, which has no resting place, which is in no temple, mosque or church, which no religion, no teacher, no philosopher, nobody can lead you to—then you will also see that this living thing is what you actually are—your anger, your brutality, your violence, your despair, the agony and sorrow you live in. In the understanding of all this is the truth, and you can understand it only if you know how to look at those things in your life. And you cannot look through an ideology, through a screen of words, through hopes and fears.

So you see that you cannot depend upon anybody. There *is* no guide, no teacher, no authority. There is only you— your relationship with others and with the world—there is nothing else. When you realise this, it either brings great despair, from which comes cynicism and bitterness, or, in facing the fact that you and nobody else are responsible for the world and for yourself, for what you think, what you feel, how you act, all self-pity goes. Normally we thrive on blaming others, which is a form of self-pity.

Can you and I, then, bring about in ourselves without any outside influence, without any persuasion, without any fear of punishment—can we bring about in the very essence of our being a total revolution, a psychological mutation, so that we are no longer brutal, violent, competitive, anxious, fearful, greedy, envious and all the rest of the manifestations of our nature which have built up the rotten society in which we live our daily lives?

It is important to understand from the very beginning that I am not formulating any philosophy or any theological structure of ideas or theological concepts. It seems to me that all ideologies are utterly idiotic. What is important is not a philosophy of life but to observe what is actually taking place in our daily life, inwardly and outwardly. If you observe very closely what is taking place and examine it, you will see that it is based on an intellectual conception, and the intellect is not the whole field of existence; it is a fragment, and a fragment, however cleverly put together, however ancient and traditional, is still a small part of existence whereas we have to deal with the totality of life. And when we look at what is taking place in the world we begin to understand that there is no outer and inner process; there is only one unitary process, it is a whole, total movement, the inner movement expressing itself as the outer and the outer reacting again on the inner. To be able to look at this seems to me all that is needed, because if we know how to look, then the whole thing becomes very clear, and to look needs no philosophy, no teacher. Nobody need tell you how to look. You just look.

Can you then, seeing this whole picture, seeing it not verbally but actually, can you easily, spontaneously, transform yourself? That is the real issue. Is it possible to bring about a complete revolution in the psyche?

I wonder what your reaction is to such a question? You may say, 'I don't want to change', and most people don't, especially those who are fairly secure socially and economically or who hold dogmatic beliefs and are content to accept themselves and things as they are or in a slightly modified form. With those people we are not concerned. Or you may say more subtly, 'Well, it's too difficult, it's not for me', in which case you will have already blocked yourself, you will have ceased to enquire and it will be no use going any further. Or else you may say, 'I see the necessity for a fundamental inward change in myself but how am I to bring it about? Please show me the way, help me towards it.' If you say that, then what you are concerned with is not change itself; you are not really interested in a fundamental revolution : you are merely searching for a method, a system, to bring about change.

If I were foolish enough to give you a system and if you were foolish enough to follow it, you would merely be copying, imitating, conforming, accepting, and when you do that you have set up in yourself the authority of another and hence there is conflict between you and that authority. You feel you must do such and such a thing because you have been told to do it and yet you are incapable of doing it. You have your own particular inclinations, tendencies and pressures which conflict with the system you think you ought to follow and therefore there is a contradiction. So you will lead a double life between the ideology of the system and the actuality of your daily existence. In trying to conform to the ideology, you suppress yourself—whereas what is actually true is not the ideology but what you are. If you try to study yourself according to another you will always remain a secondhand human being.

A man who says, 'I want to change, tell me how to', seems very earnest, very serious, but he is not. He wants an authority whom he hopes will bring about order in himself. But can authority ever bring about inward order? Order imposed from without must always breed disorder.

17

You may see the truth of this intellectually but can you actually apply it so that your mind no longer projects any authority, the authority of a book, a teacher, a wife or husband, a parent, a friend or of society? Because we have always functioned within the pattern of a formula, the formula becomes the ideology and the authority; but the moment you really see that the question, 'How can I change?' sets up a new authority, you have finished with authority for ever.

Let us state it again clearly: I see that I must change completely from the roots of my being; I can no longer depend on any tradition because tradition has brought about this colossal laziness, acceptance and obedience; I cannot possibly look to another to help me to change, not to any teacher, any God, any belief, any system, any outside pressure or influence. What then takes place?

First of all, can you reject all authority? If you can it means that you are no longer afraid. Then what happens? When you reject something false which you have been carrying about with you for generations, when you throw off a burden of any kind, what takes place? You have more energy, haven't you? You have more capacity, more drive, greater intensity and vitality. If you do not feel this, then you have not thrown off the burden, you have not discarded the dead weight of authority.

But when you have thrown it off and have this energy in which there is no fear at all—no fear of making a mistake, no fear of doing right or wrong—then is not that energy itself the mutation? We need a tremendous amount of energy and we dissipate it through fear but when there is this energy which comes from throwing off every form of fear, that energy itself produces the radical inward revolution. You do not have to do a thing about it.

So you are left with yourself, and that is the actual state

for a man to be who is very serious about all this; and as you are no longer looking to anybody or anything for help, you are already free to discover. And when there is freedom, there is energy; and when there is freedom it can never do anything wrong. Freedom is entirely different from revolt. There is no such thing as doing right or wrong when there is freedom. You *are* free and from that centre you act. And hence there is no fear, and a mind that has no fear is capable of great love. And when there is love it can do what it will.

What we are now going to do, therefore, is to learn about ourselves, not according to me or to some analyst or philosopher—because if we learn about ourselves according to someone else, we learn about *them*, not ourselves— we are going to learn what we actually are.

Having realised that we can depend on no outside authority in bringing about a total revolution within the structure of our own psyche, there is the immensely greater difficulty of rejecting our own inward authority, the authority of our own particular little experiences and accumulated opinions, knowledge, ideas and ideals. You had an experience yesterday which taught you something and what it taught you becomes a new authority—and that authority of yesterday is as destructive as the authority of a thousand years. To understand ourselves needs no authority either of yesterday or of a thousand years because we are living things, always moving, flowing, never resting. When we look at ourselves with the dead authority of yesterday we will fail to understand the living movement and the beauty and quality of that movement.

To be free of all authority, of your own and that of another, is to die to everything of yesterday, so that your mind is always fresh, always young, innocent, full of vigour

and passion. It is only in that state that one learns and observes. And for this a great deal of awareness is required, actual awareness of what is going on inside yourself, without correcting it or telling it what it should or should not be, because the moment you correct it you have established another authority, a censor.

So now we are going to investigate ourselves together—not one person explaining while you read, agreeing or disagreeing with him as you follow the words on the page, but taking a journey together, a journey of discovery into the most secret corners of our minds. And to take such a journey we must travel light; we cannot be burdened with opinions, prejudices and conclusions—all that old furniture we have collected for the last two thousand years and more. Forget all you know about yourself; forget all you have ever thought about yourself; we are going to start as if we knew nothing.

It rained last night heavily, and now the skies are beginning to clear; it is a new fresh day. Let us meet that fresh day as if it were the only day. Let us start on our journey together with all the remembrance of yesterday left behind —and begin to understand ourselves for the first time.

II

Learning About Ourselves—Simplicity and Humility
—Conditioning

IF YOU THINK it is important to know about yourself
only because I or someone else has told you it is important,
then I am afraid all communication between us comes to
an end. But if we agree that it is vital that we understand
ourselves completely, then you and I have quite a different
relationship, then we can explore together with a happy,
careful and intelligent enquiry.

I do not demand your faith; I am not setting myself up
as an authority. I have nothing to teach you—no new
philosophy, no new system, no new path to reality; there
is no path to reality any more than to truth. All authority
of any kind, especially in the field of thought and understanding, is the most destructive, evil thing. Leaders destroy
the followers and followers destroy the leaders. You have to
be your own teacher and your own disciple. You have to
question everything that man has accepted as valuable, as
necessary.

If you do not follow somebody you feel very lonely. Be
lonely then. Why are you frightened of being alone?
Because you are faced with yourself as you are and you
find that you are empty, dull, stupid, ugly, guilty and
anxious—a petty, shoddy, secondhand entity. Face the
fact; look at it, do not run away from it. The moment you
run away fear begins.

In enquiring into ourselves we are not isolating ourselves

from the rest of the world. It is not an unhealthy process. Man throughout the world is caught up in the same daily problems as ourselves, so in enquiring into ourselves we are not being in the least neurotic because there is no difference between the individual and the collective. That is an actual fact. I have created the world as I am. So don't let us get lost in this battle between the part and the whole.

I must become aware of the total field of my own self, which is the consciousness of the individual and of society. It is only then, when the mind goes beyond this individual and social consciousness, that I can become a light to myself that never goes out.

Now where do we begin to understand ourselves? Here am I, and how am I to study myself, observe myself, see what is actually taking place inside myself? I can observe myself only in relationship because all life is relationship. It is no use sitting in a corner meditating about myself. I cannot exist by myself. I exist only in relationship to people, things and ideas, and in studying my relationship to outward things and people, as well as to inward things, I begin to understand myself. Every other form of understanding is merely an abstraction and I cannot study myself in abstraction; I am not an abstract entity; therefore I have to study myself in actuality—as *I am*, not as I wish to be.

Understanding is not an intellectual process. Acquiring knowledge about yourself and learning about yourself are two different things, for the knowledge you accumulate about yourself is always of the past and a mind that is burdened with the past is a sorrowful mind. Learning about yourself is not like learning a language or a technology or a science—then you obviously have to accumulate and remember; it would be absurd to begin all over again—but in the psychological field learning about yourself is always

22

in the present and knowledge is always in the past, and as most of us live in the past and are satisfied with the past, knowledge becomes extraordinarily important to us. That is why we worship the erudite, the clever, the cunning. But if you are learning all the time, learning every minute, learning by watching and listening, learning by seeing and doing, then you will find that learning is a constant movement without the past.

If you say you will learn gradually about yourself, adding more and more, little by little, you are not studying yourself now as you are but through acquired knowledge. Learning implies a great sensitivity. There is no sensitivity if there is an idea, which is of the past, dominating the present. Then the mind is no longer quick, pliable, alert. Most of us are not sensitive even physically. We over-eat, we do not bother about the right diet, we oversmoke and drink so that our bodies become gross and insensitive; the quality of attention in the organism itself is made dull. How can there be a very alert, sensitive, clear mind if the organism itself is dull and heavy? We may be sensitive about certain things that touch us personally but to be completely sensitive to all the implications of life demands that there be no separation between the organism and the psyche. It is a total movement.

To understand anything you must live with it, you must observe it, you must know all its content, its nature, its structure, its movement. Have you ever tried living with yourself? If so, you will begin to see that yourself is not a static state, it is a fresh living thing. And to live with a living thing your mind must also be alive. And it cannot be alive if it is caught in opinions, judgements and values.

In order to observe the movement of your own mind and heart, of your whole being, you must have a free mind, not

23

a mind that agrees and disagrees, taking sides in an argument, disputing over mere words, but rather following with an intention to understand—a very difficult thing to do because most of us don't know how to look at, or listen to, our own being any more than we know how to look at the beauty of a river or listen to the breeze among the trees.

When we condemn or justify we cannot see clearly, nor can we when our minds are endlessly chattering; then we do not observe *what is*; we look only at the projections we have made of ourselves. Each of us has an image of what we think we are or what we should be, and that image, that picture, entirely prevents us from seeing ourselves as we actually are.

It is one of the most difficult things in the world to look at anything simply. Because our minds are very complex we have lost the quality of simplicity. I don't mean simplicity in clothes or food, wearing only a loin cloth or breaking a record fasting or any of that immature nonsense the saints cultivate, but the simplicity that can look directly at things without fear—that can look at ourselves as we actually are without any distortion—to say when we lie we lie, not cover it up or run away from it.

Also in order to understand ourselves we need a great deal of humility. If you start by saying, 'I know myself', you have already stopped learning about yourself; or if you say, 'There is nothing much to learn about myself because I am just a bundle of memories, ideas, experiences and traditions', then you have also stopped learning about yourself. The moment you have achieved anything you cease to have that quality of innocence and humility; the moment you have a conclusion or start examining from knowledge, you are finished, for then you are translating every living thing in terms of the old. Whereas if you have no foothold, if there is no certainty, no achievement, there is freedom to look, to achieve. And when you look with freedom it is always new. A confident man is a dead human being.

But how can we be free to look and learn when our minds from the moment we are born to the moment we die are shaped by a particular culture in the narrow pattern of the 'me'? For centuries we have been conditioned by nationality, caste, class, tradition, religion, language, education, literature, art, custom, convention, propaganda of all kinds, economic pressure, the food we eat, the climate we live in, our family, our friends, our experiences—every influence you can think of—and therefore our responses to every problem are conditioned.

Are you aware that you are conditioned? That is the first thing to ask yourself, not how to be free of your conditioning. You may never be free of it, and if you say, 'I must be free of it', you may fall into another trap of another form of conditioning. So are you aware that you are conditioned? Do you know that even when you look at a tree and say, 'That is an oak tree', or 'that is a banyan tree', the naming of the tree, which is botanical knowledge, has so conditioned your mind that the word comes between you and actually seeing the tree? To come in contact with the tree you have to put your hand on it and the word will not help you to touch it.

How do you know you are conditioned? What tells you? What tells you you are hungry?—not as a theory but the actual fact of hunger? In the same way, how do you discover the actual fact that you are conditioned? Isn't it by your reaction to a problem, a challenge? You respond to every challenge according to your conditioning and your conditioning being inadequate will always react inadequately.

When you become aware of it, does this conditioning of

25

race, religion and culture bring a sense of imprisonment? Take only one form of conditioning, nationality, become seriously, completely aware of it and see whether you enjoy it or rebel against it, and if you rebel against it, whether you want to break through all conditioning. If you are satisfied with your conditioning you will obviously do nothing about it, but if you are not satisfied when you become aware of it, you will realise that you never do anything without it. *Never!* And therefore you are always living in the past with the dead.

You will be able to see for yourself how you are conditioned only when there is a conflict in the continuity of pleasure or the avoidance of pain. If everything is perfectly happy around you, your wife loves you, you love her, you have a nice house, nice children and plenty of money, then you are not aware of your conditioning at all. But when there is a disturbance—when your wife looks at someone else or you lose your money or are threatened with war or any other pain or anxiety—then you know you are conditioned. When you struggle against any kind of disturbance or defend yourself against any outer or inner threat, then you know you are conditioned. And as most of us are disturbed most of the time, either superficially or deeply, that very disturbance indicates that we are conditioned. So long as the animal is petted he reacts nicely, but the moment he is antagonised the whole violence of his nature comes out.

We are disturbed about life, politics, the economic situation, the horror, the brutality, the sorrow in the world as well as in ourselves, and from that we realise how terribly narrowly conditioned we are. And what shall we do? Accept that disturbance and live with it as most of us do?

Get used to it as one gets used to living with a backache? Put up with it?

There is a tendency in all of us to put up with things, to get used to them, to blame them on circumstances. 'Ah, if things were right I would be different', we say, or, 'Give me the opportunity and I will fulfil myself', or, 'I am crushed by the injustice of it all', always blaming our disturbances on others or on our environment or on the economic situation.

If one gets used to disturbance it means that one's mind has become dull, just as one can get so used to beauty around one that one no longer notices it. One gets indifferent, hard and callous, and one's mind becomes duller and duller. If we do not get used to it we try to escape from it by taking some kind of drug, joining a political group, shouting, writing, going to a football match or to a temple or church or finding some other form of amusement.

Why is it that we escape from actual facts? We are afraid of death—I am just taking that as an example—and we invent all kinds of theories, hopes, beliefs, to disguise the fact of death, but the fact is still there. To understand a fact we must look at it, not run away from it. Most of us are afraid of living as well as of dying. We are afraid for our family, afraid of public opinion, of losing our job, our security, and hundreds of other things. The simple fact is that we are afraid, not that we are afraid of this or that. Now why cannot we face that fact?

You can face a fact only in the present and if you never allow it to be present because you are always escaping from it, you can never face it, and because we have cultivated a whole network of escapes we are caught in the habit of escape.

Now, if you are at all sensitive, at all serious, you will

not only be aware of your conditioning but you will also be aware of the dangers it results in, what brutality and hatred it leads to. Why, then, if you see the danger of your conditioning, don't you act? Is it because you are lazy, laziness being lack of energy? Yet you will not lack energy if you see an immediate physical danger like a snake in your path, or a precipice, or a fire. Why, then, don't you act when you see the danger of your conditioning? If you saw the danger of nationalism to your own security, wouldn't you act?

The answer is you don't see. Through an intellectual process of analysis you may see that nationalism leads to self-destruction but there is no emotional content in that. Only when there is an emotional content do you become vital.

If you see the danger of your conditioning merely as an intellectual concept, you will never do anything about it. In seeing a danger as a mere idea there is conflict between the idea and action and that conflict takes away your energy. It is only when you see the conditioning *and* the danger of it *immediately*, and as you would see a precipice, that you act. So *seeing is acting*.

Most of us walk through life inattentively, reacting unthinkingly according to the environment in which we have been brought up, and such reactions create only further bondage, further conditioning, but the moment you give your total attention to your conditioning you will see that you are free from the past completely, that it falls away from you naturally.

III

Consciousness—The Totality of Life—Awareness

WHEN YOU BECOME aware of your conditioning you
will understand the whole of your consciousness. Consciousness is the total field in which thought functions and
relationships exist. All motives, intentions, desires, pleasures,
fears, inspirations, longings, hopes, sorrows, joys are in that
field. But we have come to divide this consciousness into the
active and the dormant, the upper and lower levels—that
is, all the daily thoughts, feelings and activities on the
surface and below them the so-called subconscious, the
things with which we are not familiar, which express themselves occasionally through certain intimations, intuitions
and dreams.

We are occupied with one little corner of consciousness
which is most of our life; the rest, which we call the subconscious, with all its motives, its fears, its racial and inherited qualities, we do not even know how to get into.
Now I am asking you, is there such a thing as the subconscious at all? We use that word very freely. We have
accepted that there is such a thing and all the phrases and
jargon of the analysts and psychologists have seeped into
the language; but is there such a thing? And why is it that
we give such extraordinary importance to it? It seems to
me that it is as trivial and stupid as the conscious mind—as
narrow, bigoted, conditioned, anxious and tawdry.

So is it possible to be totally aware of the whole field of
consciousness and not merely a part, a fragment, of it?

29

If you are able to be aware of the totality, then you are functioning all the time with your total attention, not partial attention. This is important to understand because when you are being totally aware of the whole field of consciousness there is no friction. It is only when you divide consciousness, which is *all* thought, feeling and action, into different levels that there is friction.

We live in fragments. You are one thing at the office, another at home; you talk about democracy and in your heart you are autocratic; you talk about loving your neighbours, yet kill him with competition; there is one part of you working, looking, independently of the other. Are you aware of this fragmentary existence in yourself? And is it possible for a brain that has broken up its own functioning, its own thinking, into fragments—is it possible for such a brain to be aware of the whole field? Is it possible to look at the whole of consciousness completely, totally, which means to be a total human being?

If, in order to try to understand the whole structure of the 'me', the self, with all its extraordinary complexity, you go step by step, uncovering layer by layer, examining every thought, feeling and motive, you will get caught up in the analytical process which may take you weeks, months, years—and when you admit time into the process of understanding yourself, you must allow for every form of distortion because the self is a complex entity, moving, living, struggling, wanting, denying, with pressures and stresses and influences of all sorts continually at work on it. So you will discover for yourself that this is not the way; you will understand that the only way to look at yourself is totally, immediately, without time; and you can see the totality of yourself only when the mind is not fragmented. What you see in totality is the truth.

Now can you do that? Most of us cannot because most

of us have never approached the problem so seriously, because we have never really looked at ourselves. Never. We blame others, we explain things away or we are frightened to look. But when you look totally you will give your whole attention, your whole being, everything of yourself, your eyes, your ears, your nerves; you will attend with complete self-abandonment, and then there is no room for fear, no room for contradiction, and therefore no conflict.

Attention is not the same thing as concentration. Concentration is exclusion; attention, which is total awareness, excludes nothing. It seems to me that most of us are not aware, not only of what we are talking about but of our environment, the colours around us, the people, the shape of the trees, the clouds, the movement of water. Perhaps it is because we are so concerned with ourselves, with our own petty little problems, our own ideas, our own pleasures, pursuits and ambitions that we are not objectively aware. And yet we talk a great deal about awareness. Once in India I was travelling in a car. There was a chauffeur driving and I was sitting beside him. There were three gentlemen behind discussing awareness very intently and asking me questions about awareness, and unfortunately at that moment the driver was looking somewhere else and he ran over a goat, and the three gentlemen were still discussing awareness—totally unaware that they had run over a goat. When this lack of attention was pointed out to those gentlemen who were trying to be aware it was a great surprise to them.

And with most of us it is the same. We are not aware of outward things or of inward things. If you want to understand the beauty of a bird, a fly, or a leaf, or a person with all his complexities, you have to give your whole attention which is awareness. And you can give your whole attention only when you care, which means that you really love to understand—then you give your whole heart and mind to find out.

Such awareness is like living with a snake in the room; you watch its every movement, you are very, very sensitive to the slightest sound it makes. Such a state of attention is total energy; in such awareness the totality of yourself is revealed in an instant.

When you have looked at yourself so deeply you can go much deeper. When we use the word 'deeper' we are not being comparative. We think in comparisons—deep and shallow, happy and unhappy. We are always measuring, comparing. Now is there such a state as the shallow and the deep in oneself? When I say, 'My mind is shallow, petty, narrow, limited', how do I know all these things? Because I have compared my mind with your mind which is brighter, has more capacity, is more intelligent and alert. Do I know my pettiness without comparison? When I am hungry, I do not compare that hunger with yesterday's hunger. Yesterday's hunger is an idea, a memory.

If I am all the time measuring myself against you, struggling to be like you, then I am denying what I am myself. Therefore I am creating an illusion. When I have understood that comparison in any form leads only to greater illusion and greater misery, just as when I analyse myself, add to my knowledge of myself bit by bit, or identify myself with something outside myself, whether it be the State, a saviour or an ideology—when I understand that all such processes lead only to greater conformity and therefore greater conflict—when I see all this I put it completely away. Then my mind is no longer seeking. It is very important to understand this. Then my mind is no longer groping, searching, questioning. This does not mean that my mind is satisfied with things as they are, but such a mind has no illusion. Such a mind can then move in a totally different dimension. The dimension in which we usually live, the life of every day which is pain, pleasure and fear, has conditioned the mind, limited the nature of the mind, and when that pain, pleasure and fear have gone (which does not mean that you no longer have joy: joy is something entirely different from pleasure)—then the mind functions in a different dimension in which there is no conflict, no sense of 'otherness'.

Verbally we can go only so far: what lies beyond cannot be put into words because the word is not the thing. Up to now we can describe, explain, but no words or explanations can open the door. What will open the door is daily awareness and attention—awareness of how we speak, what we say, how we walk, what we think. It is like cleaning a room and keeping it in order. Keeping the room in order is important in one sense but *totally* unimportant in another. There must be order in the room but order will not open the door or the window. What will open the door is not your volition or desire. You cannot possibly invite the *other*. All that you can do is to keep the room in order, which is to be virtuous for itself, not for what it will bring. To be sane, rational, orderly. Then perhaps, if you are lucky, the window will open and the breeze will come in. Or it may not. It depends on the state of your mind. And that state of mind can be understood only by yourself, by watching it and never trying to shape it, never taking sides, never opposing, never agreeing, never justifying, never condemning, never judging—which means watching it without any choice. And out of this choiceless awareness perhaps the door will open and you will know what that dimension is in which there is no conflict and no time.

33

IV

*Pursuit of Pleasure—Desire—Perversion by Thought
—Memory—Joy*

WE SAID IN the last chapter that joy was something
entirely different from pleasure, so let us find out what is
involved in pleasure and whether it is at all possible to live
in a world that does not contain pleasure but a tremendous
sense of joy, of bliss.

We are all engaged in the pursuit of pleasure in some
form or other—intellectual, sensuous or cultural pleasure,
the pleasure of reforming, telling others what to do, of
modifying the evils of society, of doing good—the pleasure
of greater knowledge, greater physical satisfaction, greater
experience, greater understanding of life, all the clever,
cunning things of the mind—and the ultimate pleasure is,
of course, to have God.

Pleasure is the structure of society. From childhood until
death we are secretly, cunningly or obviously pursuing
pleasure. So whatever our form of pleasure is, I think we
should be very clear about it because it is going to guide
and shape our lives. It is therefore important for each one
of us to investigate closely, hesitantly and delicately this
question of pleasure, for to find pleasure, and then nourish
and sustain it, is a basic demand of life and without it
existence becomes dull, stupid, lonely and meaningless.

You may ask why then should life not be guided by
pleasure? For the very simple reason that pleasure must
bring pain, frustration, sorrow and fear, and, out of fear,

34

violence. If you want to live that way, live that way. Most of the world does, anyway, but if you want to be free from sorrow you must understand the whole structure of pleasure

To understand pleasure is not to deny it. We are not condemning it or saying it is right or wrong, but if we pursue it, let us do so with our eyes open, knowing that a mind that is all the time seeking pleasure must inevitably find its shadow, pain. They cannot be separated, although we run after pleasure and try to avoid pain.

Now, why is the mind always demanding pleasure? Why is it that we do noble and ignoble things with the undercurrent of pleasure? Why is it we sacrifice and suffer on the thin thread of pleasure? What is pleasure and how does it come into being? I wonder if any of you have asked yourself these questions and followed the answers to the very end?

Pleasure comes into being through four stages—perception, sensation, contact and desire. I see a beautiful motor car, say; then I get a sensation, a reaction, from looking at it; then I touch it or imagine touching it, and then there is the desire to own and show myself off in it. Or I see a lovely cloud, or a mountain clear against the sky, or a leaf that has just come in springtime, or a deep valley full of loveliness and splendour, or a glorious sunset, or a beautiful face, intelligent, alive, not self-conscious and therefore no longer beautiful. I look at these things with intense delight and as I observe them there is no observer but only sheer beauty like love. For a moment I am absent with all my problems, anxieties and miseries—there is only that marvellous thing. I can look at it with joy and the next moment forget it, or else the mind steps in, and then the problem begins; my mind thinks over what it has seen and thinks how beautiful it was; I tell myself I should like to see it again many times. Thought begins to compare, judge, and say, 'I must have it again tomorrow'. The continuity of an experience that has given delight for a second is sustained by thought.

It is the same with sexual desire or any other form of desire. There is nothing wrong with desire. To react is perfectly normal. If you stick a pin in me I shall react unless I am paralysed. But then thought steps in and chews over the delight and turns it into pleasure. Thought wants to repeat the experience, and the more you repeat, the more mechanical it becomes; the more you think about it, the more strength thought gives to pleasure. So thought creates and sustains pleasure through desire, and gives it continuity, and therefore the natural reaction of desire to any beautiful thing is perverted by thought. Thought turns it into a memory and memory is then nourished by thinking about it over and over again.

Of course, memory has a place at a certain level. In everyday life we could not function at all without it. In its own field it must be efficient but there is a state of mind where it has very little place. A mind which is not crippled by memory has real freedom.

Have you ever noticed that when you respond to something totally, with all your heart, there is very little memory? It is only when you do not respond to a challenge with your whole being that there is a conflict, a struggle, and this brings confusion and pleasure or pain. And the struggle breeds memory. That memory is added to all the time by other memories and it is those memories which respond. Anything that is the result of memory is old and therefore never free. There is no such thing as freedom of thought. It is sheer nonsense.

Thought is never new, for thought is the response of

36

memory, experience, knowledge. Thought, because it is old, makes this thing which you have looked at with delight and felt tremendously for the moment, old. From the old you derive pleasure, never from the new. There is no time in the new.

So if you can look at all things without allowing pleasure to creep in—at a face, a bird, the colour of a sari, the beauty of a sheet of water shimmering in the sun, or anything that gives delight—if you can look at it without wanting the experience to be repeated, then there will be no pain, no fear, and therefore tremendous joy.

It is the struggle to repeat and perpetuate pleasure which turns it into pain. Watch it in yourself. The very demand for the repetition of pleasure brings about pain, because it is not the same as it was yesterday. You struggle to achieve the same delight, not only to your aesthetic sense but the same inward quality of the mind, and you are hurt and disappointed because it is denied to you.

Have you observed what happens to you when you are denied a little pleasure? When you don't get what you want you become anxious, envious, hateful. Have you noticed when you have been denied the pleasure of drinking or smoking or sex or whatever it is—have you noticed what battles you go through? And all that is a form of fear, isn't it? You are afraid of not getting what you want or of losing what you have. When some particular faith or ideology which you have held for years is shaken or torn away from you by logic or life, aren't you afraid of standing alone? That belief has for years given you satisfaction and pleasure, and when it is taken away you are left stranded, empty, and the fear remains until you find another form of pleasure, another belief.

It seems to me so simple and because it is so simple we

refuse to see its simplicity. We like to complicate everything. When your wife turns away from you, aren't you jealous? Aren't you angry? Don't you hate the man who has attracted her? And what is all that but fear of losing something which has given you a great deal of pleasure, a companionship, a certain quality of assurance and the satisfaction of possession?

So if you understand that where there is a search for pleasure there must be pain, live that way if you want to, but don't just slip into it. If you want to end pleasure, though, which is to end pain, you must be totally attentive to the whole structure of pleasure—not cut it out as monks and sannyasis do, never looking at a woman because they think it is a sin and thereby destroying the vitality of their understanding—but seeing the whole meaning and significance of pleasure. Then you will have tremendous joy in life. You cannot think about joy. Joy is an immediate thing and by thinking about it, you turn it into pleasure. Living in the present is the instant perception of beauty and the great delight in it without seeking pleasure from it.

V

Self-concern—Craving for Position—Fears and Total
Fear—Fragmentation of Thought—Ending of Fear

Before we go any further I would like to ask you what is your fundamental, lasting interest in life? Putting all oblique answers aside and dealing with this question directly and honestly, what would you answer? Do you know?

Isn't it yourself? Anyway, that is what most of us would say if we answered truthfully. I am interested in my progress, my job, my family, the little corner in which I live, in getting a better position for myself, more prestige, more power, more domination over others and so on. I think it would be logical, wouldn't it, to admit to ourselves that that is what most of us are primarily interested in—'me' first?

Some of us would say that it is wrong to be primarily interested in ourselves. But what is wrong about it except that we seldom decently, honestly, admit it? If we do, we are rather ashamed of it. So there it is—one is fundamentally interested in oneself, and for various ideological or traditional reasons one thinks it is wrong. But what one *thinks* is irrelevant. Why introduce the factor of its being wrong? That is an idea, a concept. What is a *fact* is that one is fundamentally and lastingly interested in oneself.

You may say that it is more satisfactory to help another than to think about yourself. What is the difference? It is still self-concern. If it gives you greater satisfaction to help others, you are concerned about what will give you greater satisfaction. Why bring any ideological concept into it? Why this double thinking? Why not say, 'What I really want is satisfaction, whether in sex, or in helping others, or in becoming a great saint, scientist or politician'? It is the same process, isn't it? Satisfaction in all sorts of ways, subtle and obvious, is what we want. When we say we want freedom we want it because we think it may be wonderfully satisfying, and the ultimate satisfaction, of course, is this peculiar idea of self-realisation. What we are really seeking is a satisfaction in which there is no dissatisfaction at all.

Most of us crave the satisfaction of having a position in society because we are afraid of being nobody. Society is so constructed that a citizen who has a position of respect is treated with great courtesy, whereas a man who has no position is kicked around. Everyone in the world wants a position, whether in society, in the family or to sit on the right hand of God, and this position must be recognised by others, otherwise it is no position at all. We must always sit on the platform. Inwardly we are whirlpools of misery and mischief and therefore to be regarded outwardly as a great figure is very gratifying. This craving for position, for prestige, for power, to be recognised by society as being outstanding in some way, is a wish to dominate others, and this wish to dominate is a form of aggression. The saint who seeks a position in regard to his saintliness is as aggressive as the chicken pecking in the farmyard. And what is the cause of this aggressiveness? It is fear, isn't it?

Fear is one of the greatest problems in life. A mind that is caught in fear lives in confusion, in conflict, and therefore must be violent, distorted and aggressive. It dare not move away from its own patterns of thinking, and this breeds hypocrisy. Until we are free from fear, climb the highest mountain, invent every kind of God, we will always remain in darkness.

Living in such a corrupt, stupid society as we do, with the competitive education we receive which engenders fear, we are all burdened with fears of some kind, and fear is a dreadful thing which warps, twists and dulls our days.

There is physical fear but that is a response we have inherited from the animals. It is psychological fears we are concerned with here, for when we understand the deep-rooted psychological fears we will be able to meet the animal fears, whereas to be concerned with the animal fears first will never help us to understand the psychological fears.

We are all afraid *about* something; there is no fear in abstraction, it is always in relation *to* something. Do you know your own fears—fear of losing your job, of not having enough food or money, or what your neighbours or the public think about you, or not being a success, of losing your position in society, of being despised or ridiculed—fear of pain and disease, of domination, of never knowing what love is or of not being loved, of losing your wife or children, of death, of living in a world that is like death, of utter boredom, of not living up to the image others have built about you, of losing your faith—all these and innumerable other fears—do you know your own particular fears? And what do you usually do about them? You run away from them, don't you, or invent ideas and images to cover them? But to run away from fear is only to increase it.

One of the major causes of fear is that we do not want to face ourselves as we are. So, as well as the fears themselves, we have to examine the network of escapes we have developed to rid ourselves of them. If the mind, in which is included the brain, tries to overcome fear, to suppress it, discipline it, control it, translate it into terms of something else, there is friction, there is conflict, and that conflict is a waste of energy.

The first thing to ask ourselves then is what *is* fear and how does it arise? What do we mean by the word fear itself? I am asking myself what is fear not what I am afraid of.

I lead a certain kind of life; I think in a certain pattern; I have certain beliefs and dogmas and I don't want those patterns of existence to be disturbed because I have my roots in them. I don't want them to be disturbed because the disturbance produces a state of unknowing and I dislike that. If I am torn away from everything I know and believe, I want to be reasonably certain of the state of things to which I am going. So the brain cells have created a pattern and those brain cells refuse to create another pattern which may be uncertain. The movement from certainty to uncertainty is what I call fear.

At the actual moment as I am sitting here I am not afraid; I am not afraid in the present, nothing is happening to me, nobody is threatening me or taking anything away from me. But beyond the actual moment there is a deeper layer in the mind which is consciously or unconsciously thinking of what might happen in the future or worrying that something from the past may overtake me. So I am afraid of the past and of the future. I have divided time into the past and the future. Thought steps in, says, 'Be careful it does not happen again', or 'Be prepared for the future. The future may be dangerous for you. You have got something now but you may lose it. You may die to-morrow, your wife may run away, you may lose your job. You may never become famous. You may be lonely. You want to be quite sure of tomorrow.'

Now take your own particular form of fear. Look at it. Watch your reactions to it. Can you look at it without any movement of escape, justification, condemnation or suppression? Can you look at that fear without the word which causes the fear? Can you look at death, for instance, without the word which arouses the fear of death? The word itself brings a tremor, doesn't it, as the word love has its own tremor, its own image? Now is the image you have in your mind about death, the memory of so many deaths you have seen and the associating of yourself with those incidents—is it that image which is creating fear? Or are you actually afraid of coming to an end, not of the image creating the end? Is the word death causing you fear or the actual ending? If it is the word or the memory which is causing you fear then it is not fear at all.

You were ill two years ago, let us say, and the memory of that pain, that illness, remains, and the memory now functioning says, 'Be careful, don't get ill, again'. So the memory with its associations is creating fear, and that is not fear at all because actually at the moment you have very good health. Thought, which is always old, because thought is the response of memory and memories are always old—thought creates, in time, the feeling that you are afraid which is not an actual fact. The actual fact is that you are well. But the experience, which has remained in the mind as a memory, rouses the thought, 'Be careful, don't fall ill again'.

So we see that thought engenders one kind of fear. But is there fear at all apart from that? Is fear always the result of thought and, if it is, is there any other form of fear? We are afraid of death—that is, something that is going to happen tomorrow or the day after tomorrow, in time. There is a distance between actuality and what will be. Now thought has experienced this state; by observing death it says, 'I am going to die.' Thought creates the fear of death, and if it doesn't is there any fear at all?

43

Is fear the result of thought? If it is, thought, being always old, fear is always old. As we have said, there is no new thought. If we recognise it, it is already old. So what we are afraid of is the repetition of the old—the thought of what *has been* projecting into the future. Therefore thought is responsible for fear. This is so, you can see it for yourself. When you are confronted with something immediately there is no fear. It is only when thought comes in that there is fear.

Therefore our question now is, is it possible for the mind to live completely, totally, in the present? It is only such a mind that has no fear. But to understand this, you have to understand the structure of thought, memory and time. And in understanding it, understanding not intellectually, not verbally, but actually with your heart, your mind, your guts, you will be free from fear; then the mind can use thought without creating fear.

Thought, like memory, is, of course, necessary for daily living. It is the only instrument we have for communication, working at our jobs and so forth. Thought is the response to memory, memory which has been accumulated through experience, knowledge, tradition, time. And from this background of memory we react and this reaction is thinking. So thought is essential at certain levels but when thought projects itself psychologically as the future and the past, creating fear as well as pleasure, the mind is made dull and therefore inaction is inevitable.

So I ask myself, 'Why, why, why, do I think about the future and the past in terms of pleasure and pain, knowing that such thought creates fear? Isn't it possible for thought psychologically to stop, for otherwise fear will never end?'

One of the functions of thought is to be occupied all the time with something. Most of us want to have our minds

44

continually occupied so that we are prevented from seeing ourselves as we actually are. We are afraid to be empty. We are afraid to look at our fears.

Consciously you can be aware of your fears but at the deeper levels of your mind are you aware of them? And how are you going to find out the fears that are hidden, secret? Is fear to be divided into the conscious and the subconscious? This is a very important question. The specialist, the psychologist, the analyst, have divided fear into deep and superficial layers, but if you follow what the psychologist says or what I say, you are understanding our theories, our dogmas, our knowledge, you are not understanding yourself. You cannot understand yourself according to Freud or Jung, or according to me. Other people's theories have no importance whatever. It is of *yourself* that you must ask the question, is fear to be divided into the conscious and subconscious? Or is there only fear which you translate into different forms? There is only one desire; there is only desire. You desire. The objects of desire change, but desire is always the same. So perhaps in the same way there is only fear. You are afraid of all sorts of things but there is only one fear.

When you realise that fear cannot be divided you will see that you have put away altogether this problem of the subconscious and so have cheated the psychologists and the analysts. When you understand that fear is a single movement which expresses itself in different ways and when you see the movement and not the object to which the movement goes, then you are facing an immense question : how can you look at it without the fragmentation which the mind has cultivated?

There *is* only total fear, but how can the mind which thinks in fragments observe this total picture? Can it? We have lived a life of fragmentation, and can look at that

45

total fear only through the fragmentary process of thought. The whole process of the machinery of thinking is to break up everything into fragments: I love you and I hate you; you are my enemy, you are my friend; my peculiar idiosyncrasies and inclinations, my job, my position, my prestige, my wife, my child, my country and your country, my God and your God—all that is the fragmentation of thought. And this thought looks at the total state of fear, or tries to look at it, and reduces it to fragments. Therefore we see that the mind can look at this total fear only when there is no movement of thought.

Can you watch fear without any conclusion, without any interference of the knowledge you have accumulated about it? If you cannot, then what you are watching is the past, not fear; if you can, then you are watching fear for the first time without the interference of the past.

You can watch only when the mind is very quiet, just as you can listen to what someone is saying only when your mind is not chattering with itself, carrying on a dialogue with itself about its own problems and anxieties. Can you in the same way look at your fear without trying to resolve it, without bringing in its opposite, courage—actually look at it and not try to escape from it? When you say, 'I must control it, I must get rid of it, I must understand it', you are trying to escape from it.

You can observe a cloud or a tree or the movement of a river with a fairly quiet mind because they are not very important to you, but to watch yourself is far more difficult because there the demands are so practical, the reactions so quick. So when you are directly in contact with fear or despair, loneliness or jealousy, or any other ugly state of mind, can you look at it so completely that your mind is quiet enough to see it?

Can the mind perceive fear and not the different forms of fear—perceive total fear, not what you are afraid of? If you look merely at the details of fear or try to deal with your fears one by one, you will never come to the central issue which is to learn to live with fear.

To live with a living thing such as fear requires a mind and heart that are extraordinarily subtle, that have no conclusion and can therefore follow every movement of fear. Then if you observe and live with it—and this doesn't take a whole day, it can take a minute or a second to know the whole nature of fear—if you live with it so completely you inevitably ask, 'Who is the entity who is living with fear? Who is it who is observing fear, watching all the movements of the various forms of fear as well as being aware of the central fact of fear? Is the observer a dead entity, a static being, who has accumulated a lot of knowledge and information about himself, and is it that dead thing who is observing and living with the movement of fear? Is the observer the past or is he a living thing?' What is your answer? Do not answer me, answer yourself. Are you, the observer, a dead entity watching a living thing or are you a living thing watching a living thing? Because in the observer the two states exist.

The observer is the censor who does not want fear; the observer is the totality of all his experiences about fear. So the observer is separate from that thing he calls fear; there is space between them; he is forever trying to overcome it or escape from it and hence this constant battle between himself and fear—this battle which is such a waste of energy.

As you watch, you learn that the observer is merely a bundle of ideas and memories without any validity or substance, but that fear is an actuality and that you are trying to understand a fact with an abstraction which, of course, you cannot do. But, in fact, is the observer who says, 'I am afraid', any different from the thing observed which is fear? The observer *is* fear and when that is realised there is no longer any dissipation of energy in the effort to get rid of fear, and the time-space interval between the observer and the observed disappears. When you see that you are a part of fear, not separate from it—that *you are* fear—then you cannot do anything about it; then fear comes totally to an end.

VI

*Violence—Anger—Justification and Condemnation—
The Ideal and the Actual*

FEAR, PLEASURE, SORROW, thought and violence
are all interrelated. Most of us take pleasure in violence,
in disliking somebody, hating a particular race or group
of people, having antagonistic feelings towards others. But
in a state of mind in which all violence has come to an end
there is a joy which is very different from the pleasure of
violence with its conflicts, hatreds and fears.

Can we go to the very root of violence and be free from
it? Otherwise we shall live everlastingly in battle with each
other. If that is the way you want to live—and apparently
most people do—then carry on; if you say, 'Well, I'm
sorry, violence can never end', then you and I have no
means of communication, you have blocked yourself; but if
you say there might be a different way of living, then we
shall be able to communicate with each other.

So let us consider together, those of us who can communicate, whether it is at all possible totally to end every
form of violence in ourselves and still live in this monstrously brutal world. I think it is possible. I don't want to
have a breath of hate, jealousy, anxiety or fear in me. I
want to live completely at peace. Which doesn't mean that
I want to die. I want to live on this marvellous earth, so
full, so rich, so beautiful. I want to look at the trees, flowers,
rivers, meadows, women, boys and girls, and at the same

time live completely at peace with myself and with the world. What can I do?

If we know how to look at violence, not only outwardly in society—the wars, the riots, the national antagonisms and class conflicts—but also in ourselves, then perhaps we shall be able to go beyond it.

Here is a very complex problem. For centuries upon centuries man has been violent; religions have tried to tame him throughout the world and none of them have succeeded. So if we are going into the question we must, it seems to me, be at least very serious about it because it will lead us into quite a different domain, but if we want merely to play with the problem for intellectual entertainment we shall not get very far.

You may feel that you yourself are very serious about the problem but that as long as so many other people in the world are not serious and are not prepared to do anything about it, what is the good of your doing anything? I don't care whether they take it seriously or not. I take it seriously, that is enough. I am not my brother's keeper. I myself, as a human being, feel very strongly about this question of violence and I will see to it that in myself I am not violent —but I cannot tell you or anybody else, 'Don't be violent.' It has no meaning—unless you yourself want it. So if you yourself really want to understand this problem of violence let us continue on our journey of exploration together.

Is this problem of violence out there or here? Do you want to solve the problem in the outside world or are you questioning violence itself as it is in you? If you are free of violence in yourself the question arises, 'How am I to live in a world full of violence, acquisitiveness, greed, envy, brutality? Will I not be destroyed?' That is the inevitable question which is invariably asked. When you ask such a question it seems to me you are not actually living peacefully. If you live peacefully you will have no problem at all. You may be imprisoned because you refuse to join the army or shot because you refuse to fight—but that is not a problem; you will be shot. It is extraordinarily important to understand this.

We are trying to understand violence as a fact, not as an idea, as a fact which exists in the human being, and the human being is myself. And to go into the problem I must be *completely* vulnerable, open, to it. I must expose myself to myself—not necessarily expose myself to you because you may not be interested—but I must be in a state of mind that demands to see this thing right to the end and at no point stops and says I will go no further.

Now it must be obvious to me that I am a violent human being. I have experienced violence in anger, violence in my sexual demands, violence in hatred, creating enmity, violence in jealousy and so on—I have experienced it, I have known it, and I say to myself, 'I want to understand this whole problem not just one fragment of it expressed in war, but this aggression in man which also exists in the animals and of which I am a part.'

Violence is not merely killing another. It is violence when we use a sharp word, when we make a gesture to brush away a person, when we obey because there is fear. So violence isn't merely organised butchery in the name of God, in the name of society or country. Violence is much more subtle, much deeper, and we are inquiring into the very depths of violence.

When you call yourself an Indian or a Muslim or a Christian or a European, or anything else, you are being violent. Do you see why it is violent? Because you are separating yourself from the rest of mankind. When you separate yourself by belief, by nationality, by tradition, it breeds violence. So a man who is seeking to understand violence does not belong to any country, to any religion, to any political party or partial system; he is concerned with the total understanding of mankind.

Now there are two primary schools of thought with regard to violence, one which says, 'Violence is innate in man' and the other which says, 'Violence is the result of the social and cultural heritage in which man lives.' We are not concerned with which school we belong to—it is of no importance. What is important is the *fact* that we are violent, not the reason for it.

One of the most common expressions of violence is anger. When my wife or sister is attacked I say I am righteously angry; when my country is attacked, my ideas, my principles, my way of life, I am righteously angry. I am also angry when my habits are attacked or my petty little opinions. When you tread on my toes or insult me I get angry, or if you run away with my wife and I get jealous, that jealousy is called righteous because she is my property. And all this anger is morally justified. But to kill for my country is also justified. So when we are talking about anger, which is a part of violence, do we look at anger in terms of righteous and unrighteous anger according to our own inclinations and environmental drive, or do we see only anger? Is there righteous anger ever? Or is there only anger? There is no good influence or bad influence, only influence, but when you are influenced by something which doesn't suit me I call it an evil influence.

The moment you protect your family, your country, a bit of coloured rag called a flag, a belief, an idea, a dogma, the thing that you demand or that you hold, that very protection indicates anger. So can you look at anger without any explanation or justification, without saying, 'I must

52

protect my goods', or 'I was right to be angry', or 'How stupid of me to be angry'? Can you look at anger as if it were something by itself? Can you look at it completely objectively, which means neither defending it nor condemning it? Can you?

Can I look at you if I am antagonistic to you or if I am thinking what a marvellous person you are? I can see you only when I look at you with a certain care in which neither of these things is involved. Now, can I look at anger in the same way, which means that I am vulnerable to the problem, I do not resist it, I am watching this extraordinary phenomenon without any reaction to it?

It is very difficult to look at anger dispassionately because it is a part of me, but that is what I am trying to do. Here I am, a violent human being, whether I am black, brown, white or purple. I am not concerned with whether I have inherited this violence or whether society has produced it in me; all I am concerned with is whether it is at all possible to be free from it. To be free from violence means everything to me. It is more important to me than sex, food, position, for this thing is corrupting me. It is destroying me and destroying the world, and I want to understand it, I want to be beyond it. I feel responsible for all this anger and violence in the world. I feel responsible—it isn't just a lot of words—and I say to myself, 'I can do something only if I am beyond anger myself, beyond violence, beyond nationality'. And this feeling I have that I must understand the violence in myself brings tremendous vitality and passion to find out.

But to be beyond violence I cannot suppress it, I cannot deny it, I cannot say, 'Well, it is a part of me and that's that', or 'I don't want it'. I have to look at it, I have to study it, I must become very intimate with it and I cannot become intimate with it if I condemn it or justify it. We do

53

condemn it, though; we do justify it. Therefore I am saying, stop for the time being condemning it or justifying it.

Now, if you want to stop violence, if you want to stop wars, how much vitality, how much of yourself, do you give to it? Isn't it important to you that your children are killed, that your sons go into the army where they are bullied and butchered? Don't you care? My God, if that doesn't interest you, what does? Guarding your money? Having a good time? Taking drugs? Don't you see that this violence in yourself is destroying your children? Or do you see it only as some abstraction?

All right then, if you are interested, attend with all your heart and mind to find out. Don't just sit back and say, 'Well, tell us all about it'. I point out to you that you cannot look at anger nor at violence with eyes that condemn or justify and that if this violence is not a burning problem to you, you cannot put those two things away. So first you have to learn; you have to learn how to look at anger, how to look at your husband, your wife, your children; you have to listen to the politician, you have to learn why you are not objective, why you condemn or justify. You have to learn that you condemn and justify because it is part of the social structure you live in, your conditioning as a German or an Indian or a Negro or an American or whatever you happen to have been born, with all the dulling of the mind that this conditioning results in. To learn, to discover, something fundamental you must have the capacity to go deeply. If you have a blunt instrument, a dull instrument, you cannot go deeply. So what we are doing is sharpening the instrument, which is the mind—the mind which has been made dull by all this justifying and condemning. You can penetrate deeply only if your mind is as sharp as a needle and as strong as a diamond.

It is no good just sitting back and asking, 'How am I to get such a mind?' You have to want it as you want your next meal, and to have it you must see that what makes your mind dull and stupid is this sense of invulnerability which has built walls round itself and which is part of this condemnation and justification. If the mind can be rid of that, then you can look, study, penetrate, and perhaps come to a state that is totally aware of the whole problem.

So let us come back to the central issue—is it possible to eradicate violence in ourselves? It is a form of violence to say, 'You haven't changed, why haven't you?' I am not doing that. It doesn't mean a thing to me to convince you of *anything*. It is your life, not my life. The way you live is your affair. I am asking whether it is possible for a human being living psychologically in any society to clear violence from himself inwardly? If it is, the very process will produce a different way of living in this world.

Most of us have accepted violence as a way of life. Two dreadful wars have taught us nothing except to build more and more barriers between human beings—that is, between you and me. But for those of us who want to be rid of violence, how is it to be done? I do not think anything is going to be achieved through analysis, either by ourselves or by a professional. We might be able to modify ourselves slightly, live a little more quietly with a little more affection, but in itself it will not give total perception. But I must know how to analyse which means that in the process of analysis my mind becomes extraordinarily sharp, and it is that quality of sharpness, of attention, of seriousness, which will give total perception. One hasn't the eyes to see the whole thing at a glance; this clarity of the eye is possible only if one can see the details, *then jump.*

*

Some of us, in order to rid ourselves of violence, have used a concept, an ideal, called non-violence, and we think by having an ideal of the opposite to violence, non-violence, we can get rid of the fact, the actual—but we cannot. We have had ideals without number, all the sacred books are full of them, yet we are still violent—so why not deal with violence itself and forget the word altogether?

If you want to understand the actual you must give your whole attention, all your energy, to it. That attention and energy are distracted when you create a fictitious, ideal world. So can you completely banish the ideal? The man who is really serious, with the urge to find out what truth is, what love is, has no concept at all. He lives only in *what is.*

To investigate the fact of your own anger you must pass no judgement on it, for the moment you conceive of its opposite you condemn it and therefore you cannot see it as it is. When you say you dislike or hate someone that is a fact, although it sounds terrible. If you look at it, go into it completely, it ceases, but if you say, 'I must not hate; I must have love in my heart', then you are living in a hypocritical world with double standards. To live completely, fully, in the moment is to live with what is, the actual, without any sense of condemnation or justification—then you understand it so totally that you are finished with it. When you see clearly the problem is solved.

But can you see the face of violence clearly—the face of violence not only outside you but inside you, which means that you are totally free from violence because you have not admitted ideology through which to get rid of it? This requires very deep meditation not just a verbal agreement or disagreement.

You have now read a series of statements but have you really understood? Your conditioned mind, your way of life, the whole structure of the society in which you live, prevent you from looking at a fact and being entirely free from it *immediately*. You say, 'I will think about it; I will consider whether it is possible to be free from violence or not. I will try to be free.' That is one of the most dreadful statements you can make, 'I will try'. There is no trying, no doing your best. Either you do it or you don't do it. You are admitting time while the house is burning. The house is burning as a result of the violence throughout the world and in yourself and you say, 'Let me think about it. Which ideology is best to put out the fire?' When the house is on fire, do you argue about the colour of the hair of the man who brings the water?

VII

THE CESSATION OF violence, which we have just
been considering, does not necessarily mean a state of mind
which is at peace with itself and therefore at peace in all its
relationships.

Relationship between human beings is based on the
image-forming, defensive mechanism. In all our relationships each one of us builds an image about the other and
these two images have relationship, not the human beings
themselves. The wife has an image about the husband—
perhaps not consciously but nevertheless it is there—and
the husband has an image about the wife. One has an
image about one's country and about oneself, and we are
always strengthening these images by adding more and
more to them. And it is these images which have relationship. The actual relationship between two human beings
or between many human beings completely ends when
there is the formation of images.

Relationship based on these images can obviously never
bring about peace in the relationship because the images
are fictitious and one cannot live in an abstraction. And yet
that is what we are all doing : living in ideas, in theories, in
symbols, in images which we have created about ourselves
and others and which are not realities at all. All our
relationships, whether they be with property, ideas or

people, are based essentially on this image-forming, and hence there is always conflict.

How is it possible then to be completely at peace within ourselves and in all our relationships with others? After all, life is a movement in relationship, otherwise there is no life at all, and if that life is based on an abstraction, an idea, or a speculative assumption, then such abstract living must inevitably bring about a relationship which becomes a battlefield. So is it at all possible for man to live a completely orderly inward life without any form of compulsion, imitation, suppression or sublimation? Can he bring about such order within himself that it is a living quality not held within the framework of ideas—an inward tranquillity which knows no disturbance at any moment—not in some fantastic mythical abstract world but in the daily life of the home and the office?

I think we should go into this question very carefully because there is not one spot in our consciousness untouched by conflict. In all our relationships, whether with the most intimate person or with a neighbour or with society, this conflict exists—conflict being contradiction, a state of division, separation, a duality. Observing ourselves and our relationships to society we see that at all levels of our being there is conflict—minor or major conflict which brings about very superficial responses or devastating results.

Man has accepted conflict as an innate part of daily existence because he has accepted competition, jealousy, greed, acquisitiveness and aggression as a natural way of life. When we accept such a way of life we accept the structure of society as it is and live within the pattern of respectability. And that is what most of us are caught in because most of us want to be terribly respectable. When we examine our own minds and hearts, the way we think, the way we feel and how we act in our daily lives, we observe that as long as we conform to the pattern of society, life must be a battlefield. If we do not accept it— and no religious person can possibly accept such a society— then we will be completely free from the psychological structure of society.

Most of us are rich with the things of society. What society has created in us and what we have created in ourselves, are greed, envy, anger, hate, jealousy, anxiety—and with all these we are very rich. The various religions throughout the world have preached poverty. The monk assumes a robe, changes his name, shaves his head, enters a cell and takes a vow of poverty and chastity; in the East he has one loin cloth, one robe, one meal a day—and we all respect such poverty. But those men who have assumed the robe of poverty are still inwardly, psychologically, rich with the things of society because they are still seeking position and prestige; they belong to this order or that order, this religion or that religion; they still live in the divisions of a culture, a tradition. That is not poverty. Poverty is to be completely free of society, though one may have a few more clothes, a few more meals—good God, who cares? But unfortunately in most people there is this urge for exhibitionism.

Poverty becomes a marvellously beautiful thing when the mind is free of society. One must become poor inwardly for then there is no seeking, no asking, no desire, no— nothing! It is only this inward poverty that can see the truth of a life in which there is no conflict at all. Such a life is a benediction not to be found in any church or any temple.

How is it possible then to free ourselves from the psychological structure of society, which is to free ourselves from the essence of conflict? It is not difficult to trim and lop off certain branches of conflict, but we are asking ourselves whether it is possible to live in complete inward and therefore outward tranquillity? Which does not mean that we shall vegetate or stagnate. On the contrary, we shall become dynamic, vital, full of energy.

To understand and to be free of any problem we need a great deal of passionate and sustained energy, not only physical and intellectual energy but an energy that is not dependent on any motive, any psychological stimulus or drug. If we are dependent on any stimulus that very stimulus makes the mind dull and insensitive. By taking some form of drug we may find enough energy temporarily to see things very clearly but we revert to our former state and therefore become dependent on that drug more and more. So all stimulation, whether of the church or of alcohol or of drugs or of the written or spoken word, will inevitably bring about dependence, and that dependence prevents us from seeing clearly for ourselves and therefore from having vital energy.

We all unfortunately depend psychologically on something. Why do we depend? Why is there this urge to depend? We are taking this journey together; you are not waiting for me to tell you the causes of your dependence. If we enquire together we will both discover and therefore that discovery will be your own, and hence, being yours, it will give you vitality.

I discover for myself that I depend on something—an audience, say, which will stimulate me. I derive from that audience, from addressing a large group of people, a kind of energy. And therefore I depend on that audience, on those people, whether they agree or disagree. The more they disagree the more vitality they give me. If they agree it becomes a very shallow, empty thing. So I discover that I need an audience because it is a very stimulating thing to address people. Now why? Why do I depend? Because in myself I am shallow, in myself I have nothing, in myself I have no source which is always full and rich, vital, moving, living. So I depend. I have discovered the cause.

But will the discovery of the cause free me from being dependent? The discovery of the cause is merely intellectual, so obviously it does not free the mind from its dependency. The mere intellectual acceptance of an idea, or the emotional acquiescence in an ideology, cannot free the mind from being dependent on something which will give it stimulation. What frees the mind from dependence is seeing the whole structure and nature of stimulation and dependence and how that dependence makes the mind stupid, dull and inactive. Seeing the totality of it alone frees the mind.

So I must enquire into what it means to see totally. As long as I am looking at life from a particular point of view or from a particular experience I have cherished, or from some particular knowledge I have gathered, which is my background, which is the 'me', I cannot see totally. I have discovered intellectually, verbally, through analysis, the cause of my dependence, but whatever thought investigates must inevitably be fragmentary, so I can see the totality of something only when thought does not interfere.

Then I see the fact of my dependence; I see actually *what is*. I see it without any like or dislike; I do not want to get rid of that dependence or to be free from the cause of it. I observe it, and when there is observation of this kind I see the whole picture, not a fragment of the picture, and when the mind sees the whole picture there is freedom. Now I have discovered that there is a dissipation of energy when there is fragmentation. I have found the very source of the dissipation of energy.

You may think there is no waste of energy if you imitate, if you accept authority, if you depend on the priest, the ritual, the dogma, the party or on some ideology, but the following and acceptance of an ideology, whether it is good or bad, whether it is holy or unholy, is a fragmentary activity and therefore a cause of conflict, and conflict will inevitably arise so long as there is a division between 'what should be' and 'what is', and any conflict is a dissipation of energy.

If you put the question to yourself, 'How am I to be free from conflict?', you are creating another problem and hence you are increasing conflict, whereas if you just see it as a fact—see it as you would see some concrete object—clearly, directly—then you will understand essentially the truth of a life in which there is no conflict at all.

Let us put it another way. We are always comparing what we are with what we should be. The should-be is a projection of what we think we ought to be. Contradiction exists when there is comparison, not only with something or somebody, but with what you were yesterday, and hence there is conflict between what has been and what is. There is *what is* only when there is no comparison at all, and to live with what is, is to be peaceful. Then you can give your whole attention without any distraction to what is within yourself—whether it be despair, ugliness, brutality, fear, anxiety, loneliness—and live with it completely; then there is no contradiction and hence no conflict.

But all the time we are comparing ourselves—with those who are richer or more brilliant, more intellectual, more affectionate, more famous, more this and more that. The 'more' plays an extraordinarily important part in our lives;

this measuring ourselves all the time against something or someone is one of the primary causes of conflict.

Now why is there any comparison at all? Why do you compare yourself with another? This comparison has been taught from childhood. In every school A is compared with B, and A destroys himself in order to be like B. When you do not compare at all, when there is no ideal, no opposite, no factor of duality, when you no longer struggle to be different from what you are—what has happened to your mind? Your mind has ceased to create the opposite and has become highly intelligent, highly sensitive, capable of immense passion, because effort is a dissipation of passion —passion which is vital energy—and you cannot do anything without passion.

If you do not compare yourself with another you will be what you are. Through comparison you hope to evolve, to grow, to become more intelligent, more beautiful. But will you? The *fact* is what you are, and by comparing you are fragmenting the fact which is a waste of energy. To see what you actually are without any comparison gives you tremendous energy to look. When you can look at yourself without comparison you are beyond comparison, which does not mean that the mind is stagnant with contentment. So we see in essence how the mind wastes energy which is so necessary to understand the totality of life.

I don't want to know with whom I am in conflict; I don't want to know the peripheral conflicts of my being. What I want to know is why conflict should exist at all. When I put that question to myself I see a fundamental issue which has nothing to do with peripheral conflicts and their solutions. I am concerned with the central issue and I see—perhaps you see also?—that the very nature of desire, if not properly understood, must inevitably lead to conflict.

64

Desire is always in contradiction. I desire contradictory things—which doesn't mean that I must destroy desire, suppress, control or sublimate it—I simply see that desire itself is contradictory. It is not the objects of desire but the very nature of desire which is contradictory. And I have to understand the nature of desire before I can understand conflict. In ourselves we are in a state of contradiction, and that state of contradiction is brought about by desire— desire being the pursuit of pleasure and the avoidance of pain, which we have already been into.

So we see desire as the root of all contradiction—wanting something and not wanting it—a dual activity. When we do something pleasurable there is no effort involved at all, is there? But pleasure brings pain and then there is a struggle to avoid the pain, and that again is a dissipation of energy. Why do we have duality at all? There is, of course, duality in nature—man and woman, light and shade, night and day—but inwardly, psychologically, why do we have duality? Please think this out with me, don't wait for me to tell you. You have to exercise your own mind to find out. My words are merely a mirror in which to observe yourself. Why do we have this psychological duality? Is it that we have been brought up always to compare 'what is' with 'what should be'? We have been conditioned in what is right and what is wrong, what is good and what is bad, what is moral and what is immoral. Has this duality come into being because we believe that thinking about the opposite of violence, the opposite of envy, of jealousy, of meanness, will help us to get rid of those things? Do we use the opposite as a lever to get rid of what is? Or is it an escape from the actual?

Do you use the opposite as a means of avoiding the actual which you don't know how to deal with? Or is it

65

because you have been told by thousands of years of propaganda that you must have an ideal—the opposite of 'what is'—in order to cope with the present? When you have an ideal you think it helps you to get rid of 'what is', but it never does. You may preach non-violence for the rest of your life and all the time be sowing the seeds of violence.

You have a concept of what you should be and how you should act, and all the time you are in fact acting quite differently; so you see that principles, beliefs and ideals must inevitably lead to hypocrisy and a dishonest life. It is the ideal that creates the opposite to what is, so if you know how to be with 'what is', then the opposite is not necessary.

Trying to become like somebody else, or like your ideal, is one of the main causes of contradiction, confusion and conflict. A mind that is confused, whatever it does, at any level, will remain confused; any action born of confusion leads to further confusion. I see this very clearly; I see it as clearly as I see an immediate physical danger. So what happens? I cease to act in terms of confusion any more. Therefore inaction is complete action.

VIII

Freedom—Revolt—Solitude—Innocence—Living with Ourselves as We Are

NONE OF THE agonies of suppression, nor the brutal discipline of conforming to a pattern has led to truth. To come upon truth the mind must be completely free, without a spot of distortion.

But first let us ask ourselves if we really want to be free? When we talk of freedom are we talking of complete freedom or of freedom from some inconvenient or unpleasant or undesirable thing? We would like to be free from painful and ugly memories and unhappy experiences but keep our pleasurable, satisfying ideologies, formulas and relationships. But to keep the one without the other is impossible, for, as we have seen, pleasure is inseparable from pain.

So it is for each one of us to decide whether or not we want to be completely free. If we say we do, then we must understand the nature and structure of freedom.

Is it freedom when you are free *from* something—free from pain, free from some kind of anxiety? Or is freedom itself something entirely different? You can be free from jealousy, say, but isn't that freedom a reaction and therefore not freedom at all? You can be free from dogma very easily, by analysing it, by kicking it out, but the motive for that freedom from dogma has its own reaction because the desire to be free from a dogma may be that it is no longer fashionable or convenient. Or you can be free from nationalism because you believe in internationalism or because you feel it is no longer economically necessary to cling to this silly nationalistic dogma with its flag and all that rubbish. You can easily put that away. Or you may react against some spiritual or political leader who has promised you freedom as a result of discipline or revolt. But has such rationalism, such logical conclusion, anything to do with freedom?

If you say you are free *from* something, it is a reaction which will then become another reaction which will bring about another conformity, another form of domination. In this way you can have a chain of reactions and accept each reaction as freedom. But it is not freedom; it is merely a continuity of a modified past which the mind clings to.

The youth of today, like all youth, are in revolt against society, and that is a good thing in itself, but revolt is not freedom because when you revolt it is a reaction and that reaction sets up its own pattern and you get caught in that pattern. You think it is something new. It is not; it is the old in a different mould. Any social or political revolt will inevitably revert to the good old bourgeois mentality.

Freedom comes only when you see and act, never through revolt. The seeing is the acting and such action is as instantaneous as when you see danger. Then there is no cerebration, no discussion or hesitation; the danger itself compels the act, and therefore to see is to act and to be free.

Freedom is a state of mind—not freedom *from* something but a sense of freedom, a freedom to doubt and question everything and therefore so intense, active and vigorous that it throws away every form of dependence, slavery, conformity and acceptance. Such freedom implies being completely alone. But can the mind brought up in a culture so dependent on environment and its own tendencies ever find that freedom which is complete solitude and in which there is no leadership, no tradition and no authority?

This solitude is an inward state of mind which is not dependent on any stimulus or any knowledge and is not the result of any experience or conclusion. Most of us, inwardly, are never alone. There is a difference between isolation, cutting oneself off, and aloneness, solitude. We all know what it is to be isolated—building a wall around oneself in order never to be hurt, never to be vulnerable, or cultivating detachment which is another form of agony, or living in some dreamy ivory tower of ideology. Aloneness is something quite different.

You are never alone because you are full of all the memories, all the conditioning, all the mutterings of yesterday; your mind is never clear of all the rubbish it has accumulated. To be alone you must die to the past. When you are alone, totally alone, not belonging to any family, any nation, any culture, any particular continent, there is that sense of being an outsider. The man who is completely alone in this way is innocent and it is this innocency that frees the mind from sorrow.

We carry about with us the burden of what thousands of people have said and the memories of all our misfortunes. To abandon all that totally is to be alone, and the mind that is alone is not only innocent but young—not in time or age, but young, innocent, alive at whatever age—and only such a mind can see that which is truth and that which is not measurable by words.

In this solitude you will begin to understand the necessity of living with yourself as you are, not as you think you should be or as you have been. See if you can look at yourself without any tremor, any false modesty, any fear, any justification or condemnation—just live with yourself as you actually are.

It is only when you live with something intimately that you begin to understand it. But the moment you get used to it—get used to your own anxiety or envy or whatever it is—you are are no longer living with it. If you live by a river, after a few days you do not hear the sound of the water any more, or if you have a picture in the room which you see every day you lose it after a week. It is the same with the mountains, the valleys, the trees—the same with your family, your husband, your wife. But to live with something like jealousy, envy or anxiety you must never get used to it, never accept it. You must care for it as you would care for a newly planted tree, protect it against the sun, against the storm. You must care for it, not condemn it or justify it. Therefore you begin to love it. When you care for it, you are beginning to love it. It is not that you love being envious or anxious, as so many people do, but rather that you care for watching.

So can you—can you and I—live with what we actually are, knowing ourselves to be dull, envious, fearful, believing we have tremendous affection when we have not, getting easily hurt, easily flattered and bored—can we live with all that, neither accepting it nor denying it, but just observing it without becoming morbid, depressed or elated?

Now let us ask ourselves a further question. Is this freedom, this solitude, this coming into contact with the whole structure of what we are in ourselves—is it to be come upon through time? That is, is freedom to be achieved through a gradual process? Obviously not, because as soon as you introduce time you are enslaving yourself more and more. You cannot become free gradually. It is not a matter of time.

The next question is, can you become conscious of that freedom? If you say, 'I am free', then you are not free. It is like a man saying, 'I am happy'. The moment he says,

'I am happy' he is living in a memory of something that has gone. Freedom can only come about naturally, not through wishing, wanting, longing. Nor will you find it by creating an image of what you think it is. To come upon it the mind has to learn to look at life, which is a vast movement, without the bondage of time, for freedom lies beyond the field of consciousness.

IX

Time—Sorrow—Death

I AM TEMPTED TO repeat a story about a great disciple going to God and demanding to be taught truth. This poor God says, 'My friend, it is such a hot day, please get me a glass of water.' So the disciple goes out and knocks on the door of the first house he comes to and a beautiful young lady opens the door. The disciple falls in love with her and they marry and have several children. Then one day it begins to rain, and keeps on raining, raining, raining —the torrents are swollen, the streets are full, the houses are being washed away. The disciple holds on to his wife and carries his children on his shoulders and as he is being swept away he calls out, 'Lord, please save me', and the Lord says, 'Where is that glass of water I asked for?'

It is rather a good story because most of us think in terms of time. Man lives by time. Inventing the future has been his favourite game of escape.

We think that changes in ourselves can come about in time, that order in ourselves can be built up little by little, added to day by day. But time doesn't bring order or peace, so we must stop thinking in terms of gradualness. This means that there is no tomorrow for us to be peaceful in. We have to be orderly on the instant.

When there is real danger time disappears, doesn't it? There is immediate action. But we do not see the danger of many of our problems and therefore we invent time as a means of overcoming them. Time is a deceiver as it doesn't do a thing to help us bring about a change in ourselves. Time is a movement which man has divided into past, present and future, and as long as he divides it he will always be in conflict.

Is learning a matter of time? We have not learnt after all these thousands of years that there is a better way to live than by hating and killing each other. The problem of time is a very important one to understand if we are to resolve this life which we have helped to make as monstrous and meaningless as it is.

The first thing to understand is that we can look at time only with that freshness and innocency of mind which we have already been into. We are confused about our many problems and lost in that confusion. Now if one is lost in a wood, what is the first thing one does? One stops, doesn't one? One stops and looks round. But the more we are confused and lost in life the more we chase around, searching, asking, demanding, begging. So the first thing, if I may suggest it, is that you completely stop inwardly. And when you do stop inwardly, psychologically, your mind becomes very peaceful, very clear. Then you can really look at this question of time.

Problems exist only in time, that is when we meet an issue incompletely. This incomplete coming together with the issue creates the problem. When we meet a challenge partially, fragmentarily, or try to escape from it—that is, when we meet it without complete attention—we bring about a problem. And the problem continues so long as we continue to give it incomplete attention, so long as we hope to solve it *one of these days.*

Do you know what time is? Not by the watch, not chronological time, but psychological time? It is the interval between idea and action. An idea is for self-protection obviously; it is the idea of being secure. Action is always immediate; it is not of the past or of the future; to act must always be in the present, but action is so dangerous, so uncertain, that we conform to an idea which we hope will give us a certain safety.

Do look at this in yourself. You have an idea of what is right or wrong, or an ideological concept about yourself and society, and according to that idea you are going to act. Therefore the action is in conformity with that idea, approximating to the idea, and hence there is always conflict. There is the idea, the interval and action. And in that interval is the whole field of time. That interval is essentially thought. When you think you will be happy tomorrow, then you have an image of yourself achieving a certain result in time. Thought, through observation, through desire, and the continuity of that desire sustained by further thought, says, 'Tomorrow I shall be happy. Tomorrow I shall have success. Tomorrow the world will be a beautiful place.' So thought creates that interval which is time.

Now we are asking, can we put a stop to time? Can we live so completely that there is no tomorrow for thought to think about? Because time is sorrow. That is, yesterday or a thousand yesterday's ago, you loved, or you had a companion who has gone, and that memory remains and you are thinking about that pleasure and that pain—you are looking back, wishing, hoping, regretting, so thought, going over it again and again, breeds this thing we call sorrow and gives continuity to time.

So long as there is this interval of time which has been bred by thought, there must be sorrow, there must be continuity of fear. So one asks oneself can this interval come to an end? If you say, 'Will it ever end?', then it is already an idea, something you want to achieve, and therefore you have an interval and you are caught again.

Now take the question of death which is an immense problem to most people. You know death, there it is walking every day by your side. Is it possible to meet it so completely that you do not make a problem of it at all? In order to meet it in such a way all belief, all hope, all fear about it must come to an end, otherwise you are meeting this extraordinary thing with a conclusion, an image, with a premeditated anxiety, and therefore you are meeting it with time.

Time is the interval between the observer and the observed. That is, the observer, you, is afraid to meet this thing called death. You don't know what it means; you have all kinds of hopes and theories about it; you believe in reincarnation or resurrection, or in something called the soul, the atman, a spiritual entity which is timeless and which you call by different names. Now have you found out for yourself whether there is a soul? Or is it an idea that has been handed down to you? *Is* there something permanent, continuous, which is beyond thought? If thought can think about it, it is within the field of thought and therefore it cannot be permanent because there is nothing permanent within the field of thought. To discover that nothing is permanent is of tremendous importance for only then is the mind free, then you can look, and in that there is great joy.

You cannot be frightened of the unknown because you do not know what the unknown is and so there is nothing to be frightened of. Death is a word, and it is the word, the image, that creates fear. So can you look at death without the image of death? As long as the image exists from which springs thought, thought must always create fear.

Then you either rationalise your fear of death and build a resistance against the inevitable or you invent innumerable beliefs to protect you from the fear of death. Hence there is a gap between you and the thing of which you are afraid. In this time-space interval there must be conflict which is fear, anxiety and self-pity. Thought, which breeds the fear of death, says, 'Let's postpone it, let's avoid it, keep it as far away as possible, let's not think about it'—but you *are* thinking about it. When you say, 'I won't think about it', you have already thought out how to avoid it. You are frightened of death because you have postponed it.

We have separated living from dying, and the interval between the living and the dying is fear. That interval, that time, is created by fear. Living is our daily torture, daily insult, sorrow and confusion, with occasional opening of a window over enchanted seas. That is what we call living, and we are afraid to die, which is to end this misery. We would rather cling to the known than face the unknown—the known being our house, our furniture, our family, our character, our work, our knowledge, our fame, our loneliness, our gods—that little thing that moves around incessantly within itself with its own limited pattern of embittered existence.

We think that living is always in the present and that dying is something that awaits us at a distant time. But we have never questioned whether this battle of everyday life is living at all. We want to know the truth about reincarnation, we want proof of the survival of the soul, we listen to the assertion of clairvoyants and to the conclusions of psychical research, but we never ask, *never*, how to live —to live with delight, with enchantment, with beauty every day. We have accepted life as it is with all its agony and despair and have got used to it, and think of death as something to be carefully avoided. But death is extraordinarily like life when we know how to live. You cannot live without dying. You cannot live if you do not die psychologically every minute. This is not an intellectual paradox. To live completely, wholly, every day as if it were a new loveliness, there must be dying to everything of yesterday, otherwise you live mechanically, and a mechanical mind can never know what love is or what freedom is.

Most of us are frightened of dying because we don't know what it means to live. We don't know how to live, therefore we don't know how to die. As long as we are frightened of life we shall be frightened of death. The man who is not frightened of life is not frightened of being completely insecure for he understands that inwardly, psychologically, there is no security. When there is no security there is an endless movement and then life and death are the same. The man who lives without conflict, who lives with beauty and love, is not frightened of death because to love is to die.

If you die to everything you know, including your family, your memory, everything you have felt, then death is a purification, a rejuvenating process; then death brings innocence and it is only the innocent who are passionate, not the people who believe or who want to find out what happens after death.

To find out actually what takes place when you die you must die. This isn't a joke. You must die—not physically but psychologically, inwardly, die to the things you have cherished and to the things you are bitter about. If you have died to one of your pleasures, the smallest or the greatest, naturally, without any enforcement or argument, then you will know what it means to die. To die is to have a mind that is completely empty of itself, empty of its daily longings, pleasures and agonies. Death is a renewal, a mutation, in which thought does not function at all because thought is old. When there is death there is something totally new. Freedom from the known is death, and then you are living.

X

Love

THE DEMAND TO be safe in relationship inevitably breeds sorrow and fear. This seeking for security is inviting insecurity. Have you ever found security in any of your relationships? Have you? Most of us want the security of loving and being loved, but is there love when each one of us is seeking his own security, his own particular path? We are not loved because we don't know how to love.

What is love? The word is so loaded and corrupted that I hardly like to use it. Everybody talks of love—every magazine and newspaper and every missionary talks everlastingly of love. I love my country, I love my king, I love some book, I love that mountain, I love pleasure, I love my wife, I love God. Is love an idea? If it is, it can be cultivated, nourished, cherished, pushed around, twisted in any way you like. When you say you love God what does it mean? It means that you love a projection of your own imagination, a projection of yourself clothed in certain forms of respectability according to what you think is noble and holy; so to say, 'I love God', is absolute nonsense. When you worship God you are worshipping yourself—and that is not love.

Because we cannot solve this human thing called love we run away into abstractions. Love may be the ultimate solution to all man's difficulties, problems and travails, so how are we going to find out what love is? By merely defining it? The church has defined it one way, society another, and there are all sorts of deviations and perversions. Adoring someone, sleeping with someone, the emotional exchange, the companionship—is that what we mean by love? That has been the norm, the pattern, and it has become so tremendously personal, sensuous, and limited that religions have declared that love is something much more than this. In what they call human love they see there is pleasure, competition, jealousy, the desire to possess, to hold, to control and to interfere with another's thinking, and knowing the complexity of all this they say there must be another kind of love, divine, beautiful, untouched, uncorrupted.

Throughout the world, so-called holy men have maintained that to look at a woman is something totally wrong: they say you cannot come near to God if you indulge in sex, therefore they push it aside although they are eaten up with it. But by denying sexuality they put out their eyes and cut out their tongues for they deny the whole beauty of the earth. They have starved their hearts and minds; they are dehydrated human beings; they have banished beauty because beauty is associated with woman.

Can love be divided into the sacred and the profane, the human and the divine, or is there only love? Is love of the one and not of the many? If I say, 'I love you', does that exclude the love of the other? Is love personal or impersonal? Moral or immoral? Family or non-family? If you love mankind can you love the particular? Is love sentiment? Is love emotion? Is love pleasure and desire? All these questions indicate, don't they, that we have ideas about love, ideas about what it should or should not be, a pattern or a code developed by the culture in which we live.

So to go into the question of what love is we must first

free it from the encrustation of centuries, put away all ideals and ideologies of what it should or should not be. To divide anything into what should be and what is, is the most deceptive way of dealing with life.

Now how am I going to find out what this flame is which we call love—not how to express it to another but what it means in itself? I will first reject what the church, what society, what my parents and friends, what every person and every book has said about it because I want to find out for myself what it is. Here is an enormous problem that involves the whole of mankind, there have been a thousand ways of defining it and I myself am caught in some pattern or other according to what I like or enjoy at the moment—so shouldn't I, in order to understand it, first free myself from my own inclinations and prejudices? I am confused, torn by my own desires, so I say to myself, 'First clear up your own confusion. Perhaps you may be able to discover what love is through what it is not.'

The government says, 'Go and kill for the love of your country'. Is that love? Religion says, 'Give up sex for the love of God'. Is that love? Is love desire? Don't say no. For most of us it is—desire with pleasure, the pleasure that is derived through the senses, through sexual attachment and fulfilment. I am not against sex, but see what is involved in it. What sex gives you momentarily is the total abandonment of yourself, then you are back again with your turmoil, so you want a repetition over and over again of that state in which there is no worry, no problem, no self. You say you love your wife. In that love is involved sexual pleasure, the pleasure of having someone in the house to look after your children, to cook. You depend on her; she has given you her body, her emotions, her encouragement, a certain feeling of security and well-being. Then she turns away from you; she gets bored or goes off with someone else, and your whole emotional balance is destroyed, and this disturbance, which you don't like, is called jealousy. There is pain in it, anxiety, hate and violence. So what you are really saying is, 'As long as you belong to me I love you but the moment you don't I begin to hate you. As long as I can rely on you to satisfy my demands, sexual and otherwise, I love you, but the moment you cease to supply what I want I don't like you.' So there is antagonism between you, there is separation, and when you feel separate from another there is no love. But if you can live with your wife without thought creating all these contradictory states, these endless quarrels in yourself, then perhaps—*perhaps*—you will know what love is. Then you are completely free and so is she, whereas if you depend on her for all your pleasure you are a slave to her. So when one loves there must be freedom, not only from the other person but from oneself.

This belonging to another, being psychologically nourished by another, depending on another—in all this there must always be anxiety, fear, jealousy, guilt, and so long as there is fear there is no love; a mind ridden with sorrow will never know what love is; sentimentality and emotionalism have nothing whatsoever to do with love. And so love is not to do with pleasure and desire.

Love is not the product of thought which is the past. Thought cannot possibly cultivate love. Love is not hedged about and caught in jealousy, for jealousy is of the past. Love is always active present. It is not 'I will love' or 'I have loved'. If you know love you will not follow anybody. Love does not obey. When you love there is neither respect nor disrespect.

Don't you know what it means really to love somebody —to love without hate, without jealousy, without anger,

82

without wanting to interfere with what he is doing or thinking, without condemning, without comparing—don't you know what it means? Where there is love is there comparison? When you love someone with all your heart, with all your mind, with all your body, with your entire being, is there comparison? When you totally abandon yourself to that love there is not the other.

Does love have responsibility and duty, and will it use those words? When you do something out of duty is there any love in it? In duty there is no love. The structure of duty in which the human being is caught is destroying him. So long as you are compelled to do something because it is your duty you don't love what you are doing. When there is love there is no duty and no responsibility.

Most parents unfortunately think they are responsible for their children and their sense of responsibility takes the form of telling them what they should do and what they should not do, what they should become and what they should not become. The parents want their children to have a secure position in society. What they call responsibility is part of that respectability they worship; and it seems to me that where there is respectability there is no order; they are concerned only with becoming a perfect bourgeois. When they prepare their children to fit into society they are perpetuating war, conflict and brutality. Do you call that care and love?

Really to care is to care as you would for a tree or a plant, watering it, studying its needs, the best soil for it, looking after it with gentleness and tenderness—but when you prepare your children to fit into society you are preparing them to be killed. If you loved your children you would have no war.

When you lose someone you love you shed tears—are your tears for yourself or for the one who is dead? Are you crying for yourself or for another? Have you ever cried for another? Have you ever cried for your son who is killed on the battlefield? You have cried, but do those tears come out of self-pity or have you cried because a human being has been killed? If you cry out of self-pity your tears have no meaning because you are concerned about yourself. If you are crying because you are bereft of one in whom you have invested a great deal of affection, it was not really affection. When you cry for your brother who dies cry for *him*. It is very easy to cry for yourself because he is gone. Apparently you are crying because your heart is touched, but it is not touched for him, it is only touched by self-pity and self-pity makes you hard, encloses you, makes you dull and stupid.

When you cry for yourself, is it love—crying because you are lonely, because you have been left, because you are no longer powerful—complaining of your lot, your environment—always *you* in tears? If you understand this, which means to come in contact with it as directly as you would touch a tree or a pillar or a hand, then you will see that sorrow is self-created, sorrow is created by thought, sorrow is the outcome of time. I had my brother three years ago, now he is dead, now I am lonely, aching, there is no one to whom I can look for comfort or companionship, and it brings tears to my eyes.

You can see all this happening inside yourself if you watch it. You can see it fully, completely, in one glance, not take analytical time over it. You can see in a moment the whole structure and nature of this shoddy little thing called 'me', my tears, my family, my nation, my belief, my religion—all that ugliness, it is all inside you. When you see it with your heart, not with your mind, when you see it from the very bottom of your heart, then you have the key that will end sorrow.

Sorrow and love cannot go together, but in the Christian world they have idealised suffering, put it on a cross and worshipped it, implying that you can never escape from suffering except through that one particular door, and this is the whole structure of an exploiting religious society.

So when you ask what love is, you may be too frightened to see the answer. It may mean complete upheaval; it may break up the family; you may discover that you do not love your wife or husband or children—do you?—you may have to shatter the house you have built, you may never go back to the temple.

But if you still want to find out, you will see that fear is not love, dependence is not love, jealousy is not love, possessiveness and domination are not love, responsibility and duty are not love, self-pity is not love, the agony of not being loved is not love, love is not the opposite of hate any more than humility is the opposite of vanity. So if you can eliminate all these, not by forcing them but by washing them away as the rain washes the dust of many days from a leaf, then perhaps you will come upon this strange flower which man always hungers after.

If you have not got love—not just in little drops but in abundance—if you are not filled with it—the world will go to disaster. You know intellectually that the unity of mankind is essential and that love is the only way, but who is going to teach you how to love? Will any authority, any method, any system, tell you how to love? If anyone tells you, it is not love. Can you say, 'I will practise love. I will sit down day after day and think about it. I will practise being kind and gentle and force myself to pay attention to others'? Do you mean to say that you can discipline yourself to love, exercise the will to love? When you exercise discipline and will to love, love goes out of the window. By

85

practising some method or system of loving you may become extraordinarily clever or more kindly or get into a state of non-violence, but that has nothing whatsoever to do with love.

In this torn desert world there is no love because pleasure and desire play the greatest roles, yet without love your daily life has no meaning. And you cannot have love if there is no beauty. Beauty is not something you see—not a beautiful tree, a beautiful picture, a beautiful building or a beautiful woman. There is beauty only when your heart and mind know what love is. Without love and that sense of beauty there is no virtue, and you know very well that, do what you will, improve society, feed the poor, you will only be creating more mischief, for without love there is only ugliness and poverty in your own heart and mind. But when there is love and beauty, whatever you do is right, whatever you do is in order. If you know how to love, then you can do what you like because it will solve all other problems.

So we reach the point: can the mind come upon love without discipline, without thought, without enforcement, without any book, any teacher or leader—come upon it as one comes upon a lovely sunset?

It seems to me that one thing is absolutely necessary and that is passion without motive—passion that is not the result of some commitment or attachment, passion that is not lust. A man who does not know what passion is will never know love because love can come into being only when there is total self-abandonment.

A mind that is seeking is not a passionate mind and to come upon love without seeking it is the only way to find it —to come upon it unknowingly and not as the result of any effort or experience. Such a love, you will find, is not of time; such a love is both personal and impersonal, is both the one and the many. Like a flower that has perfume you can smell it or pass it by. That flower is for everybody *and* for the one who takes trouble to breathe it deeply and look at it with delight. Whether one is very near in the garden, or very far away, it is the same to the flower because it is full of that perfume and therefore it is sharing with everybody.

Love is something that is new, fresh, alive. It has no yesterday and no tomorrow. It is beyond the turmoil of thought. It is only the innocent mind which knows what love is, and the innocent mind can live in the world which is not innocent. To find this extraordinary thing which man has sought endlessly through sacrifice, through worship, through relationship, through sex, through every form of pleasure and pain, is only possible when thought comes to understand itself and comes naturally to an end. Then love has no opposite, then love has no conflict.

You may ask, 'If I find such a love, what happens to my wife, my children, my family? They must have security.' When you put such a question you have never been outside the field of thought, the field of consciousness. When once you have been outside that field you will never ask such a question because then you will know what love is in which there is no thought and therefore no time. You may read this mesmerised and enchanted, but actually to go beyond thought and time—which means going beyond sorrow—is to be aware that there is a different dimension called love.

But you don't know how to come to this extraordinary fount—so what do you do? If you don't know what to do, you do nothing, don't you? Absolutely nothing. Then inwardly you are completely silent. Do you understand what that means? It means that you are not seeking, not wanting, not pursuing; there is no centre at all. Then there is love.

XI

To Look and to Listen—Art—Beauty—Austerity—
Images—Problems—Space

WE HAVE BEEN enquiring into the nature of love and
have come to a point, I think, which needs much greater
penetration, a much greater awareness of the issue. We
have discovered that for most people love means comfort,
security, a guarantee for the rest of their lives of continuous
emotional satisfaction. Then someone like me comes along
and says, 'Is that really love?' and questions you and asks
you to look inside yourself. And you try not to look because
it is very disturbing—you would rather discuss the soul
or the political or economic situation—but when you are
driven into a corner to look, you realise that what you have
always thought of as love is not love at all; it is a mutual
gratification, a mutual exploitation.

When I say, 'Love has no tomorrow and no yesterday',
or, 'When there is no centre then there is love', it has reality
for me but not for you. You may quote it and make it into
a formula but that has no validity. You have to see it for
yourself, but to do so there must be freedom to look, freedom from all condemnation, all judgement all agreeing or
disagreeing.

Now, to look is one of the most difficult things in life—
or to listen—to look and listen are the same. If your eyes
are blinded with your worries, you cannot see the beauty of
the sunset. Most of us have lost touch with nature. Civilisa-

tion is tending more and more towards large cities; we are becoming more and more an urban people, living in crowded apartments and having very little space even to look at the sky of an evening and morning, and therefore we are losing touch with a great deal of beauty. I don't know if you have noticed how few of us look at a sunrise or a sunset or the moonlight or the reflection of light on water.

Having lost touch with nature we naturally tend to develop intellectual capacities. We read a great many books, go to a great many museums and concerts, watch television and have many other entertainments. We quote endlessly from other people's ideas and think and talk a great deal about art. Why is it that we depend so much upon art? Is it a form of escape, of stimulation? If you are directly in contact with nature; if you watch the movement of a bird on the wing, see the beauty of every movement of the sky, watch the shadows on the hills or the beauty on the face of another, do you think you will want to go to any museum to look at any picture? Perhaps it is because you do not know how to look at all the things about you that you resort to some form of drug to stimulate you to see better.

There is a story of a religious teacher who used to talk every morning to his disciples. One morning he got on to the platform and was just about to begin when a little bird came and sat on the window sill and began to sing, and sang away with full heart. Then it stopped and flew away and the teacher said, 'The sermon for this morning is over'.

It seems to me that one of our greatest difficulties is to see for ourselves really clearly, not only outward things but inward life. When we say we see a tree or a flower or a person, do we actually see them? Or do we merely see the image that the word has created? That is, when you look at a tree or at a cloud of an evening full of light and delight, do you actually see it, not only with your eyes and intellectually, but totally, completely?

Have you ever experimented with looking at an objective thing like a tree without any of the associations, any of the knowledge you have acquired about it, without any prejudice, any judgement, any words forming a screen between you and the tree and preventing you from seeing it as it actually is? Try it and see what actually takes place when you observe the tree with all your being, with the totality of your energy. In that intensity you will find that there is no observer at all; there is only attention. It is when there is inattention that there is the observer and the observed. When you are looking at something with complete attention there is no space for a conception, a formula or a memory. This is important to understand because we are going into something which requires very careful investigation.

It is only a mind that looks at a tree or the stars or the sparkling waters of a river with complete self-abandonment that knows what beauty is, and when we are actually *seeing* we are in a state of love. We generally know beauty through comparison or through what man has put together, which means that we attribute beauty to some object. I see what I consider to be a beautiful building and that beauty I appreciate because of my knowledge of architecture and by comparing it with other buildings I have seen. But now I am asking myself, 'Is there a beauty without object?' When there is an observer who is the censor, the experiencer, the thinker, there is no beauty because beauty is something external, something the observer looks at and judges, but when there is no observer—and this demands a great deal of meditation, of enquiry—then there is beauty without the object.

Beauty lies in the total abandonment of the observer and the observed and there can be self-abandonment only when there is total austerity—not the austerity of the priest with its harshness, its sanctions, rules and obedience—not austerity in clothes, ideas, food and behaviour—but the austerity of being totally simple which is complete humility. Then there is no achieving, no ladder to climb; there is only the first step and the first step is the everlasting step.

Say you are walking by yourself or with somebody and you have stopped talking. You are surrounded by nature and there is no dog barking, no noise of a car passing or even the flutter of a bird. You are completely silent and nature around you is also wholly silent. In that state of silence both in the observer and the observed—when the observer is not translating what he observes into thought—in that silence there is a different quality of beauty. There is neither nature nor the observer. There is a state of mind wholly, completely, alone; it is alone—not in isolation—alone in stillness and that stillness is beauty. When you love, is there an observer? There is an observer only when love is desire and pleasure. When desire and pleasure are not associated with love, then love is intense. It is, like beauty, something totally new every day. As I have said, it has no yesterday and no tomorrow.

It is only when we see without any preconception, any image, that we are able to be in direct contact with anything in life. All our relationships are really imaginary—that is, based on an image formed by thought. If I have an image about you and you have an image about me, naturally we don't see each other at all as we actually are. What we see is the images we have formed about each other which prevent us from being in contact, and that is why our relationships go wrong.

When I say I know you, I mean I knew you yesterday. I do not know you actually *now*. All I know is my image of you. That image is put together by what you have said in praise of me or to insult me, what you have done to me— it is put together by all the memories I have of you—and your image of me is put together in the same way, and it is those images which have relationship and which prevent us from really communing with each other.

Two people who have lived together for a long time have an image of each other which prevents them from really being in relationship. If we understand relationship we can co-operate but co-operation cannot possibly exist through images, through symbols, through ideological conceptions. Only when we understand the true relationship between each other is there a possibility of love, and love is denied when we have images. Therefore it is important to understand, not intellectually but *actually* in your daily life, how you have built images about your wife, your husband, your neighbour, your child, your country, your leaders, your politicians, your gods—you have nothing but images.

These images create the space between you and what you observe and in that space there is conflict, so what we are going to find out now together is whether it is possible to be free of the space we create, not only outside ourselves but in ourselves, the space which divides people in all their relationships.

Now the very attention you give to a problem is the energy that solves that problem. When you give your complete attention—I mean with everything in you—there is no observer at all. There is only the state of attention which is total energy, and that total energy is the highest form of intelligence. Naturally that state of mind must be completely silent and that silence, that stillness, comes when there is total attention, not disciplined stillness. That total silence in which there is neither the observer nor the thing observed is the highest form of a religious mind. But what takes place in that state cannot be put into words because what is said in words is not the fact. To find out for yourself you have to go through it.

Every problem is related to every other problem so that if you can solve one problem completely—it does not matter what it is—you will see that you are able to meet all other problems easily and resolve them. We are talking, of course, of psychological problems. We have already seen that a problem exists only in time, that is when we meet the issue incompletely. So not only must we be aware of the nature and structure of the problem and see it completely, but meet it as it arises and resolve it immediately so that it does not take root in the mind. If one allows a problem to endure for a month or a day, or even for a few minutes, it distorts the mind. So is it possible to meet a problem immediately without any distortion and be immediately, completely, free of it and not allow a memory, a scratch on the mind, to remain? These memories are the images we carry about with us and it is these images which meet this extraordinary thing called life and therefore there is a contradiction and hence conflict. Life is very real—life is not an abstraction—and when you meet it with images there are problems.

Is it possible to meet every issue without this space-time interval, without the gap between oneself and the thing of which one is afraid? It is possible only when the observer has no continuity, the observer who is the builder of the image, the observer who is a collection of memories and ideas, who is a bundle of abstractions.

When you look at the stars there is you who are looking at the stars in the sky; the sky is flooded with brilliant stars, there is cool air, and there is you, the observer, the experiencer, the thinker, you with your aching heart, you, the centre, creating space. You will never understand about the space between yourself and the stars, yourself and your wife or husband, or friend, because you have never looked without the image, and that is why you do not know what beauty is or what love is. You talk about it, you write about it, but you have never known it except perhaps at rare intervals of total self-abandonment. So long as there is a centre creating space around itself there is neither love nor beauty. When there is no centre and no circumference then there is love. And when you love you *are* beauty.

When you look at a face opposite, you are looking from a centre and the centre creates the space between person and person, and that is why our lives are so empty and callous. You cannot cultivate love or beauty, nor can you invent truth, but if you are all the time aware of what you are doing, you can cultivate awareness and out of that awareness you will begin to see the nature of pleasure, desire and sorrow and the utter loneliness and boredom of man, and then you will begin to come upon that thing called 'the space'.

When there is space between you and the object you are observing you will know there is no love, and without love, however hard you try to reform the world or bring about a new social order or however much you talk about improvements, you will only create agony. So it is up to you. There is no leader, there is no teacher, there is nobody to tell you what to do. You are alone in this mad brutal world.

XII

The Observer and the Observed

PLEASE GO ON with me a little further. It may be rather complex, rather subtle, but please go on with it.

Now, when I build an image about you or about anything, I am able to watch that image, so there is the image and the observer of the image. I see someone, say, with a red shirt on and my immediate reaction is that I like it or that I don't like it. The like or dislike is the result of my culture, my training, my associations, my inclinations, my acquired and inherited characteristics. It is from that centre that I observe and make my judgement, and thus the observer is separate from the thing he observes.

But the observer is aware of more than one image; he creates thousands of images. But is the observer different from these images? Isn't he just another image? He is always adding to and subtracting from what he is; he is a living thing all the time weighing, comparing, judging, modifying and changing as a result of pressures from outside and within—living in the field of consciousness which is his own knowledge, influence and innumerable calculations. At the same time when you look at the observer, who is yourself, you see that he is made up of memories, experiences, accidents, influences, traditions and infinite varieties of suffering, all of which are the past. So the observer is both the past and the present, and tomorrow is waiting and that is also a part of him. He is half alive and half dead and with this death and life he is looking, with the dead and living leaf. And in that state of mind, which is within the field of time, you (the observer) look at fear, at jealousy, at war, at the family (that ugly enclosed entity called the family) and try to solve the problem of the thing observed which is the challenge, the new; you are always translating the new in terms of the old and therefore you are everlastingly in conflict.

One image, as the observer, observes dozens of other images around himself and inside himself, and he says, 'I like this image, I'm going to keep it' or 'I don't like that image so I'll get rid of it', but the observer himself has been put together by the various images which have come into being through reaction to various other images. So we come to a point where we can say, 'The observer is also the image, only he has separated himself and observes. This observer who has come into being through various other images thinks himself permanent and between himself and the images he has created there is a division, a time interval. This creates conflict between himself and the images he believes to be the cause of his troubles. So then he says, "I must get rid of this conflict", but the very desire to get rid of the conflict creates another image.'

Awareness of all this, which is real meditation, has revealed that there is a central image put together by all the other images, and this central image, the observer, is the censor, the experiencer, the evaluator, the judge who wants to conquer or subjugate the other images or destroy them altogether. The other images are the result of judgements, opinions and conclusions by the observer, and the observer is the result of all the other images—therefore the observer *is* the observed.

So awareness has revealed the different states of one's

mind, has revealed the various images and the contradiction between the images, has revealed the resulting conflict and the despair at not being able to do anything about it and the various attempts to escape from it. All this has been revealed through cautious hesitant awareness, and then comes the awareness that the observer *is* the observed. It is not a superior entity who becomes aware of this, it is not a higher self (the superior entity, the higher self, are merely inventions, further images); it is the awareness itself which had revealed that the observer is the observed.

If you ask yourself a question, who is the entity who is going to receive the answer? And who is the entity who is going to enquire? If the entity is part of consciousness, part of thought, then it is incapable of finding out. What it can find out is only a state of awareness. But if in that state of awareness there is still an entity who says, 'I must be aware, I must practise awareness', that again is another image.

This awareness that the observer is the observed is not a process of identification with the observed. To identify ourselves with something is fairly easy. Most of us identify ourselves with something—with our family, our husband or wife, our nation—and that leads to great misery and great wars. We are considering something entirely different and we must understand it not verbally but in our core, right at the root of our being. In ancient China before an artist began to paint anything—a tree, for instance—he would sit down in front of it for days, months, years, it didn't matter how long, until he *was* the tree. He did not identify himself with the tree but he was the tree. This means that there was no space between him and the tree, no space between the observer and the observed, no experiencer experiencing the beauty, the movement, the shadow, the depth of a leaf, the quality of colour. He was totally the tree, and in that state only could he paint.

Any movement on the part of the observer, if he has not realised that the observer is the observed, creates only another series of images and again he is caught in them. But what takes place when the observer is aware that the observer is the observed? Go slowly, go very slowly, because it is a very complex thing we are going into now. What takes place? The observer does not act at all. The observer has always said, 'I must do something about these images, I must suppress them or give them a different shape'; he is always active in regard to the observed, acting and reacting passionately or casually, and this action of like and dislike on the part of the observer is called positive action—'I like, therefore I must hold. I dislike therefore I must get rid of.' But when the observer realises that the thing about which he is acting is *himself*, then there is no conflict between himself and the image. He *is that*. He is not separate from that. When he was separate, he did, or tried to do, something about it, but when the observer realises that he *is* that, then there is no like or dislike and conflict ceases.

For what is he to do? If something *is* you, what can you do? You cannot rebel against it or run away from it or even accept it. It *is there*. So all action that is the outcome of reaction to like and dislike has come to an end.

Then you will find that there is an awareness that has become tremendously alive. It is not bound to any central issue or to any image—and from that intensity of awareness there is a different quality of attention and therefore the mind—because the mind is this awareness—has become extraordinarily sensitive and highly intelligent.

XIII

What is Thinking?—Ideas and Action—Challenge—
Matter—The Beginning of Thought

LET US NOW go into the question of what is thinking,
the significance of that thought which must be exercised
with care, logic and sanity (for our daily work) and that
which has no significance at all. Unless we know the two
kinds, we cannot possibly understand something much
deeper which thought cannot touch. So let us try to understand this whole complex structure of what is thinking,
what is memory, how thought originates, how thought con-
ditions all our actions; and in understanding all this we
shall perhaps come across something which thought has
never discovered, which thought cannot open the door to.

Why has thought become so important in all our lives—
thought being ideas, being the response to the accumulated
memories in the brain cells? Perhaps many of you have not
even asked such a question before, or if you have you may
have said, 'It's of very little importance—what is important
is emotion.' But I don't see how you can separate the two.
If thought doesn't give continuity to feeling, feeling dies
very quickly. So why in our daily lives, in our grinding,
boring, frightened lives, has thought taken on such in-
ordinate importance? Ask yourself as I am asking myself—
why is one a slave to thought—cunning, clever, thought
which can organise, which can start things, which has in-
vented so much, bred so many wars, created so much fear,
so much anxiety, which is forever making images and

chasing its own tail—thought which has enjoyed the pleasure of yesterday and given that pleasure continuity in the present and also in the future—thought which is always active, chattering, moving, constructing, taking away, adding, supposing?

Ideas have become far more important to us than action —ideas so cleverly expressed in books by the intellectuals in every field. The more cunning, the more subtle, those ideas are the more we worship them and the books that contain them. We *are* those books, we *are* those ideas, so heavily conditioned are we by them. We are forever discussing ideas and ideals and dialectically offering opinions. Every religion has its dogma, its formula, its own scaffold to reach the gods, and when inquiring into the beginning of thought we are questioning the importance of this whole edifice of ideas. We have separated ideas from action because ideas are always of the past and action is always the present—that is, living is always the present. We are afraid of living and therefore the past, as ideas, has become so important to us.

It is really extraordinarily interesting to watch the operation of one's own thinking, just to observe how one thinks, where that reaction we call thinking, springs from. Obviously from memory. Is there a beginning to thought at all? If there is, can we find out its beginning—that is, the beginning of memory, because if we had no memory we would have no thought?

We have seen how thought sustains and gives continuity to a pleasure that we had yesterday and how thought also sustains the reverse of pleasure which is fear and pain, so the experiencer, who is the thinker, *is* the pleasure and the pain and also the entity who gives nourishment to the pleasure and pain. The thinker separates pleasure from pain. He doesn't see that in the very demand for pleasure he is inviting pain and fear. Thought in human relationships is always demanding pleasure which it covers by different words like loyalty, helping, giving, sustaining, serving. I wonder why we want to serve? The petrol station offers good service. What do those words mean, to help, to give, to serve? What is it all about? Does a flower full of beauty, light and loveliness say, 'I am giving, helping, serving'? It *is*! And because it is not trying to do anything it covers the earth.

Thought is so cunning, so clever, that it distorts everything for its own convenience. Thought in its demand for pleasure brings its own bondage. Thought is the breeder of duality in all our relationships : there is violence in us which gives us pleasure but there is also the desire for peace, the desire to be kind and gentle. This is what is going on all the time in all our lives. Thought not only breeds this duality in us, this contradiction, but it also accumulates the innumerable memories we have had of pleasure and pain, and from these memories it is reborn. So thought is the past, thought is always old, as I have already said.

As every challenge is met in terms of the past—a challenge being always new—our meeting of the challenge will always be totally inadequate, hence contradiction, conflict and all the misery and sorrow we are heir to. Our little brain is in conflict *whatever* it does. Whether it aspires, imitates, conforms, suppresses, sublimates, takes drugs to expand itself—*whatever* it does—it is in a state of conflict and will produce conflict.

Those who think a great deal are very materialistic because thought is matter. Thought is matter as much as the floor, the wall, the telephone, are matter. Energy functioning in a pattern becomes matter. There is energy and there is matter. That is all life is. We may think thought is not matter but it is. Thought is matter as an ideology. Where there is energy it becomes matter. Matter and energy are interrelated. The one cannot exist without the other, and the more harmony there is between the two, the more balance, the more active the brain cells are. Thought has set up this pattern of pleasure, pain, fear, and has been functioning inside it for thousands of years and cannot break the pattern because it has created it.

A new fact cannot be seen by thought. It can be understood later by thought, verbally, but the understanding of a new fact is not reality to thought. Thought can never solve any psychological problem. However clever, however cunning, however erudite, whatever the structure thought creates through science, through an electronic brain, through compulsion or necessity, thought is never new and therefore it can never answer any tremendous question. The old brain cannot solve the enormous problem of living.

Thought is crooked because it can invent anything and see things that are not there. It can perform the most extraordinary tricks, and therefore it cannot be depended upon. But if you understand the whole structure of how you think, why you think, the words you use, the way you behave in your daily life, the way you talk to people, the way you treat people, the way you walk, the way you eat —if you are aware of all these things then your mind will not deceive you, then there is nothing to be deceived. The mind then is not something that demands, that subjugates; it becomes extraordinarily quiet, pliable, sensitive, alone, and in that state there is no deception whatsoever.

Have you ever noticed that when you are in a state of complete attention the observer, the thinker, the centre, the 'me', comes to an end? In that state of attention thought begins to wither away.

If one wants to see a thing very clearly, one's mind must be very quiet, without all the prejudices, the chattering, the dialogue, the images, the pictures—all that must be put aside to look. And it is only in silence that you can observe the beginning of thought—not when you are searching, asking questions, waiting for a reply. So it is only when you are completely quiet, right through your being, having put that question, 'What is the beginning of thought?', that you will begin to see, out of that silence, how thought takes shape.

If there is an awareness of how thought begins then there is no need to control thought. We spend a great deal of time and waste a great deal of energy all through our lives, not only at school, trying to control our thoughts—'This is a good thought, I must think about it a lot. This is an ugly thought, I must suppress it.' There is a battle going on all the time between one thought and another, one desire and another, one pleasure dominating all other pleasures. But if there is an awareness of the beginning of thought, then there is no contradiction in thought.

Now when you hear a statement like 'Thought is always old' or 'Time is sorrow', thought begins to translate it and interpret it. But the translation and interpretation are based on yesterday's knowledge and experience, so you will invariably translate according to your conditioning. But if you look at those statements and do not interpret them all but just give them your complete attention (not concentration) you will find there is neither the observer nor the observed, neither the thinker nor the thought. Don't say, 'Which began first?' That is a clever argument which leads nowhere. You can observe in yourself that as long as there is no thought—which doesn't mean a state of amnesia, of blankness—as long as there is no thought derived from memory, experience or knowledge, which are all of the past, there is no thinker at all. This is not a philosophical or mystical affair. We are dealing with actual facts, and you will see, if you have gone this far in the journey, that you will respond to a challenge, not with the old brain, but totally anew.

XIV

*The Burdens of Yesterday—The Quiet Mind—Com-
munication — Achievement —Discipline — Silence
—Truth and Reality*

IN THE LIFE we generally lead there is very little
solitude. Even when we are alone our lives are crowded by
so many influences, so much knowledge, so many memories
of so many experiences, so much anxiety, misery and conflict that our minds become duller and duller, more and
more insensitive, functioning in a monotonous routine. Are
we ever alone? Or are we carrying with us all the burdens
of yesterday?

There is a rather nice story of two monks walking from
one village to another and they come upon a young girl
sitting on the bank of a river, crying. And one of the monks
goes up to her and says, 'Sister, what are you crying
about?' She says, 'You see that house over there across the
river? I came over this morning early and had no trouble
wading across but now the river has swollen and I can't
get back. There is no boat.' 'Oh,' says the monk, 'that is no
problem at all', and he picks her up and carries her across
the river and leaves her on the other side. And the two
monks go on together. After a couple of hours, the other
monk says, 'Brother, we have taken a vow never to touch
a woman. What you have done is a terrible sin. Didn't you
have pleasure, a great sensation, in touching a woman?'
and the other monk replies, 'I left her behind two hours
ago. You are still carrying her, aren't you?'

That is what we do. We carry our burdens all the time; we never die to them, we never leave them behind. It is only when we give complete attention to a problem and solve it *immediately*—never carrying it over to the next day, the next minute—that there is solitude. Then, even, if we live in a crowded house or are in a bus, we have solitude. And that solitude indicates a fresh mind, an innocent mind.

To have inward solitude and space is very important because it implies freedom to be, to go, to function, to fly. After all, goodness can only flower in space just as virtue can flower only when there is freedom. We may have political freedom but inwardly we are not free and therefore there is no space. No virtue, no quality that is worth while, can function or grow without this vast space within oneself. And space and silence are necessary because it is only when the mind is alone, uninfluenced, untrained, not held by infinite varieties of experience, that it can come upon something totally new.

One can see directly that it is only when the mind is silent that there is a possibility of clarity. The whole purpose of meditation in the East is to bring about such a state of mind—that is, to control thought, which is the same as constantly repeating a prayer to quieten the mind and in that state hoping to understand one's problems. But unless one lays the foundation, which is to be free from fear, free from sorrow, anxiety and all the traps one lays for oneself, I do not see how it is possible for a mind to be actually quiet. This is one of the most difficult things to communicate. Communication between us implies, doesn't it, that not only must you understand the words I am using but that we must both, you and I, be intense at the same time, not a moment later or a moment sooner and capable of meeting each other on the same level? And such communication is not possible when you are interpreting what you are reading according to your own knowledge, pleasure or opinions, or when you are making a tremendous effort to comprehend.

It seems to me that one of the greatest stumbling blocks in life is this constant struggle to reach, to achieve, to acquire. We are trained from childhood to acquire and to achieve—the very brain cells themselves create and demand this pattern of achievement in order to have physical security, but psychological security is not within the field of achievement. We demand security in all our relationships, attitudes and activities but, as we have seen, there is actually no such thing as security. To find out for yourself that there is no form of security in any relationship—to realise that psychologically there is nothing permanent—gives a totally different approach to life. It is essential, of course, to have outward security—shelter, clothing, food—but that outward security is destroyed by the demand for psychological security.

Space and silence are necessary to go beyond the limitations of consciousness, but how can a mind which is so endlessly active in its self-interest be quiet? One can discipline it, control it, shape it, but such torture does not make the mind quiet; it merely makes it dull. Obviously the mere pursuit of the ideal of having a quiet mind is valueless because the more you force it the more narrow and stagnant it becomes. Control in any form, like suppression, produces only conflict. So control and outward discipline are not the way, nor has an *un*disciplined life any value.

Most of our lives are outwardly disciplined by the demands of society, by the family, by our own suffering, by our own experience, by conforming to certain ideological or factual patterns—and that form of discipline is the most deadening thing. Discipline must be without control, without suppression, without any form of fear. How is this discipline to come about? It is not discipline first and then freedom; freedom is at the very beginning, not at the end. To understand this freedom, which is the freedom from the conformity of discipline, is discipline itself. The very act of learning is discipline (after all the root meaning of the word discipline is to learn), the very act of learning becomes clarity. To understand the whole nature and structure of control, suppression and indulgence demands attention. You don't have to impose discipline in order to study it, but the very act of studying brings about its own discipline in which there is no suppression.

In order to deny authority (we are talking of psychological authority, not the law)—to deny the authority of all religious organisations, traditions and experience, one has to see why one normally obeys—actually study it. And to study it there must be freedom from condemnation, justification, opinion or acceptance. Now we cannot accept authority and yet study it—that is impossible. To study the whole psychological structure of authority within ourselves there must be freedom. And when we are studying we are denying the whole structure, and when we do deny, that very denial is the light of the mind that is free from authority. Negation of everything that has been considered worthwhile, such as outward discipline, leadership, idealism, is to study it; then that very act of studying is not only discipline but the negative of it, and the very denial is a positive act. So we are negating all those things that are considered important to bring about the quietness of the mind.

Thus we see it is not control that leads to quietness. Nor is the mind quiet when it has an object which is so absorbing that it gets lost in that object. This is like giving a child an interesting toy; he becomes very quiet, but remove the toy and he returns to his mischief-making. We all have our toys which absorb us and we think we are very quiet but if a man is dedicated to a certain form of activity, scientific, literary or whatever it is, the toy merely absorbs him and he is not really quiet at all.

The only silence we know is the silence when noise stops, the silence when thought stops—but that is not silence. Silence is something entirely different, like beauty, like love. And this silence is not the product of a quiet mind, it is not the product of the brain cells which have understood the whole structure and say, 'For God's sake be quiet'; then the brain cells themselves produce the silence and that is not silence. Nor is silence the outcome of attention in which the observer is the observed; then there is no friction, but that is not silence.

You are waiting for me to describe what this silence is so that you can compare it, interpret it, carry it away and bury it. It cannot be described. What can be described is the known, and the freedom from the known can come into being only when there is a dying every day to the known, to the hurts, the flatteries, to all the images you have made, to all your experiences—dying every day so that the brain cells themselves become fresh, young, innocent. But that innocency, that freshness, that quality of tenderness and gentleness, does not produce love; it is not the quality of beauty or silence.

That silence which is not the silence of the ending of noise is only a small beginning. It is like going through a small hole to an enormous, wide, expansive ocean, to an immeasurable, timeless state. But this you cannot understand verbally unless you have understood the whole structure of consciousness and the meaning of pleasure, sorrow and despair, and the brain cells themselves have become quiet. Then perhaps you may come upon that mystery which nobody can reveal to you and nothing can destroy. A living mind is a still mind, a living mind is a mind that has no centre and therefore no space and time. Such a mind is limitless and that is the only truth, that is the only reality.

Experience—Satisfaction—Duality—Meditation

WE ALL WANT experiences of some kind—the mystical experience, the religious experience, the sexual experience, the experience of having a great deal of money, power, position, domination. As we grow older we may have finished with the demands of our physical appetites but then we demand wider, deeper and more significant experiences, and we try various means to obtain them—expanding our consciousness, for instance, which is quite an art, or taking various kinds of drugs. This is an old trick which has existed from time immemorial—chewing a piece of leaf or experimenting with the latest chemical to bring about a temporary alteration in the structure of the brain cells, a greater sensitivity and heightened perception which give a semblance of reality. This demand for more and more experiences shows the inward poverty of man. We think that through experiences we can escape from ourselves but these experiences are conditioned by what we are. If the mind is petty, jealous, anxious, it may take the very latest form of drug but it will still see only its own little creation, its own little projections from its own conditioned background.

Most of us demand completely satisfying, lasting experiences which cannot be destroyed by thought. So behind this demand for experience is the desire for satisfaction, and the demand for satisfaction dictates the experience, and therefore we have not only to understand this whole business of satisfaction but also the thing that is experienced. To have some great satisfaction is a great pleasure; the more lasting, deep and wide the experience the more pleasurable it is, so pleasure dictates the form of experience we demand, and pleasure is the measure by which we measure the experience. Anything measurable is within the limits of thought and is apt to create illusion. You can have marvellous experiences and yet be completely deluded. You will inevitably see visions according to your conditioning; you will see Christ or Buddha or whoever you happen to believe in, and the greater a believer you are the stronger will be your visions, the projections of your own demands and urges.

So if in seeking something fundamental, such as what is truth, pleasure is the measure, you have already projected what that experience will be and therefore it is no longer valid.

What do we mean by experience? Is there anything new or original in experience? Experience is a bundle of memories responding to a challenge and it can respond only according to its background, and the cleverer you are at interpreting the experience the more it responds. So you have to question not only the experience of another but your own experience. If you don't recognise an experience it isn't an experience at all. Every experience has already been experienced or you wouldn't recognise it. You recognise an experience as being good, bad, beautiful, holy and so on according to your conditioning, and therefore the recognition of an experience must inevitably be old.

When we demand an experience of reality—as we all do, don't we?—to experience it we must know it and the

XV

moment we recognise it we have already projected it and therefore it is not real because it is still within the field of thought and time. If thought can think about reality it cannot be reality. We cannot recognise a *new* experience. It is impossible. We recognise only something we have already known and therefore when we say we have had a new experience it is not new at all. To seek further experience through expansion of consciousness, as is being done through various psychedelic drugs, is still within the field of consciousness and therefore very limited.

So we have discovered a fundamental truth, which is that a mind that is seeking, craving, for wider and deeper experience is a very shallow and dull mind because it lives always with its memories.

Now if we didn't have any experience at all, what would happen to us? We depend on experiences, on challenges, to keep us awake. If there were no conflicts within ourselves, no changes, no disturbances, we would all be fast asleep. So challenges are necessary for most of us; we think that without them our minds will become stupid and heavy, and therefore we depend on a challenge, an experience, to give us more excitement, more intensity, to make our minds sharper. But in fact this dependence on challenges and experiences to keep us awake, only makes our minds duller—it doesn't really keep us awake at all. So I ask myself, is it possible to keep awake totally, not peripherally at a few points of my being, but totally awake without any challenge or any experience? This implies a great sensitivity, both physical and psychological; it means I have to be free of all demands, for the moment I demand I will experience. And to be free of demand and satisfaction necessitates investigation into myself and an understanding of the whole nature of demand.

Demand is born out of duality: 'I am unhappy and I

must be happy'. In that very demand that I must be happy is unhappiness. When one makes an effort to be good, in that very goodness is its opposite, evil. Everything affirmed contains its own opposite, and effort to overcome strengthens that against which it strives. When you demand an experience of truth or reality, that very demand is born out of your discontent with what is, and therefore the demand creates the opposite. And in the opposite there is what *has been*. So one must be free of this incessant demand, otherwise there will be no end to the corridor of duality. This means knowing yourself so completely that the mind is no longer seeking.

Such a mind does not demand experience; it cannot ask for a challenge or know a challenge; it does not say, 'I am asleep' or 'I am awake'. It is completely what it is. Only the frustrated, narrow, shallow mind, the conditioned mind, is always seeking the more. Is it possible then to live in this world without the more—without this everlasting comparison? Surely it is? But one has to find out for oneself.

Investigation into this whole question is meditation. That word had been used both in the East and the West in a most unfortunate way. There are different schools of meditation, different methods and systems. There are systems which say, 'Watch the movement of your big toe, watch it, watch it, watch it'; there are other systems which advocate sitting in a certain posture, breathing regularly or practising awareness. All this is utterly mechanical. Another method gives you a certain word and tells you that if you go on repeating it you will have some extraordinary transcendental experience. This is sheer nonsense. It is a form of self-hypnosis. By repeating Amen or Om or Coca-Cola indefinitely you will obviously have a certain experience because by repetition the mind becomes quiet. It is a well known phenomenon which has been practised for thousands of years in India—Mantra Yoga it is called. By repetition you can induce the mind to be gentle and soft but it is still a petty, shoddy, little mind. You might as well put a piece of stick you have picked up in the garden on the mantelpiece and give it a flower every day. In a month you will be worshipping it and not to put a flower in front of it will become a sin.

Meditation is not following any system; it is not constant repetition and imitation. Meditation is not concentration. It is one of the favourite gambits of some teachers of meditation to insist on their pupils learning concentration—that is, fixing the mind on one thought and driving out all other thoughts. This is a most stupid, ugly thing, which any schoolboy can do because he is forced to. It means that all the time you are having a battle between the insistence that you must concentrate on the one hand and your mind on the other which wanders away to all sorts of other things, whereas you should be attentive to every movement of the mind wherever it wanders. When your mind wanders off it means you are interested in something else.

Meditation demands an astonishingly alert mind; meditation is the understanding of the totality of life in which every form of fragmentation has ceased. Meditation is not control of thought, for when thought is controlled it breeds conflict in the mind, but when you understand the structure and origin of thought, which we have already been into, then thought will not interfere. That very understanding of the structure of thinking is its own discipline which is meditation.

Meditation is to be aware of every thought and of every feeling, never to say it is right or wrong but just to watch it and move with it. In that watching you begin to understand the whole movement of thought and feeling. And out of this awareness comes silence. Silence put together by thought is stagnation, is dead, but the silence that comes when thought has understood its own beginning, the nature of itself, understood how all thought is never free but always old—this silence is meditation in which the meditator is entirely absent, for the mind has emptied itself of the past.

If you have read this book for a whole hour attentively, that is meditation. If you have merely taken away a few words and gathered a few ideas to think about later, then it is no longer meditation. Meditation is a state of mind which looks at everything with complete attention, totally, not just parts of it. And no one can teach you how to be attentive. If any system teaches you how to be attentive, then you are attentive to the system and that is not attention. Meditation is one of the greatest arts in life—perhaps *the* greatest, and one cannot possibly learn it from anybody, that is the beauty of it. It has no technique and therefore no authority. When you learn about yourself, watch yourself, watch the way you walk, how you eat, what you say, the gossip, the hate, the jealousy—if you are aware of all that in yourself, without any choice, that is part of meditation.

So meditation can take place when you are sitting in a bus or walking in the woods full of light and shadows, or listening to the singing of birds or looking at the face of your wife or child.

In the understanding of meditation there is love, and love is not the product of systems, of habits, of following a method. Love cannot be cultivated by thought. Love can perhaps come into being when there is complete silence, a silence in which the meditator is entirely absent; and the mind can be silent only when it understands its own movement as thought and feeling. To understand this movement of thought and feeling there can be no condemnation in observing it. To observe in such a way is the discipline, and that kind of discipline is fluid, free, not the discipline of conformity.

XVI

*Total Revolution—The Religious Mind—Energy—
Passion*

WHAT WE HAVE been concerned with all through this
book is the bringing about in ourselves, and therefore in our
lives, of a total revolution that has nothing whatsoever to
do with the structure of society as it is. Society as it is, is a
horrifying thing with its endless wars of aggression, whether
that aggression be defensive or offensive. What we need is
something totally new—a revolution, a mutation, in the
psyche itself. The old brain cannot possibly solve the human
problem of relationship. The old brain is Asiatic, European,
American or African, so what we are asking ourselves is
whether it is possible to bring about a mutation in the brain
cells themselves?

Let us ask ourselves again, now that we have come to
understand ourselves better, is it possible for a human being
living an ordinary everyday life in this brutal, violent, ruthless world—a world which is becoming more and more
efficient and therefore more and more ruthless—is it possible
for him to bring about a revolution not only in his outward
relationships but in the whole field of his thinking, feeling,
acting and reacting?

Every day we see or read of appalling things happening
in the world as the result of violence in man. You may say,
'I can't do anything about it', or, 'How can I influence the
world?' I think you can tremendously influence the world
if in yourself you are not violent, if you lead actually every

day a peaceful life—a life which is not competitive, ambitious, envious—a life which does not create enmity. Small fires can become a blaze. We have reduced the world to its present state of chaos by our self-centred activity, by our prejudices, our hatreds, our nationalism, and when we say we cannot do anything about it, we are accepting disorder in ourselves as inevitable. We have splintered the world into fragments and if we ourselves are broken, fragmented, our relationship with the world will also be broken. But if, when we act, we act totally, then our relationship with the world undergoes a tremendous revolution.

After all, any movement which is worth while, any action which has any deep significance, must begin with each one of us. I must change first; I must see what is the nature and structure of my relationship with the world—and in the very *seeing* is the doing; therefore I, as a human being living in the world, bring about a different quality, and that quality, it seems to me, is the quality of the religious mind.

The religious mind is something entirely different from the mind that believes in religion. You cannot be religious and yet be a Hindu, a Muslim, a Christian, a Buddhist. A religious mind does not seek at all, it cannot experiment with truth. Truth is not something dictated by your pleasure or pain, or by your conditioning as a Hindu or whatever religion you belong to. The religious mind is a state of mind in which there is no fear and therefore no belief whatsoever but only *what is—what actually is*.

In the religious mind there is that state of silence we have already examined which is not produced by thought but is the outcome of awareness, which is meditation when the meditator is entirely absent. In that silence there is a state of energy in which there is no conflict. Energy is action and movement. All action is movement and all action is energy. All desire is energy. All feeling is energy. All thought is energy. All living is energy. All life is energy. If that energy is allowed to flow without any contradiction, without any friction, without any conflict, then that energy is boundless, endless. When there is no friction there are no frontiers to energy. It is friction which gives energy limitations. So, having once seen this, why is it that the human being always brings friction into energy? Why does he create friction in this movement which we call life? Is pure energy, energy without limitation, just an idea to him? Does it have no reality?

We need energy not only to bring about a total revolution in ourselves but also in order to investigate, to look, to act. And as long as there is friction of any kind in any of our relationships, whether between husband and wife, between man and man, between one community and another or one country and another or one ideology and another—if there is any inward friction or any outward conflict in any form, however subtle it may be—there is a waste of energy.

As long as there is a time interval between the observer and the observed it creates friction and therefore there is a waste of energy. That energy is gathered to its highest point when the observer is the observed, in which there is no time interval at all. Then there will be energy without motive and it will find its own channel of action because then the 'I' does not exist.

We need a tremendous amount of energy to understand the confusion in which we live, and the feeling, 'I must understand', brings about the vitality to find out. But finding out, searching, implies time, and, as we have seen, gradually to uncondition the mind is not the way. Time is not the way. Whether we are old or young it is *now* that the whole process of life can be brought into a different dimension. Seeking the opposite of what we are is not the way either, nor is the artificial discipline imposed by a system, a teacher, a philosopher or priest—all that is so very childish. When we realise this, we ask ourselves is it possible to break through this heavy conditioning of centuries immediately and not enter into another conditioning—to be free, so that the mind can be altogether new, sensitive, alive, aware, intense, capable? That is our problem. There is no other problem because when the mind is made new it can tackle any problem. That is the only question we have to ask ourselves.

But we do not ask. We want to be told. One of the most curious things in the structure of our psyche is that we all want to be told because we are the result of the propaganda of ten thousand years. We want to have our thinking confirmed and corroborated by another, whereas to ask a question is to ask it of yourself. What I say has very little value. You will forget it the moment you shut this book, or you will remember and repeat certain phrases, or you will compare what you have read here with some other book— but you will not face your own life. And that is all that matters—your life, yourself, your pettiness, your shallowness, your brutality, your violence, your greed, your ambition, your daily agony and endless sorrow—that is what you have to understand and nobody on earth or in heaven is going to save you from it but yourself.

Seeing everything that goes on in your daily life, your daily activities—when you pick up a pen, when you talk, when you go out for a drive or when you are walking alone in the woods—can you with one breath, with one look, know yourself very simply as you are? When you know yourself as you are, then you understand the whole structure of man's endeavour, his deceptions, his hypocrisies, his search. To do this you must be tremendously honest with yourself throughout your being. When you act according to your principles you are being dishonest because when you act according to what you think you ought to be you are not what you are. It is a brutal thing to have ideals. If you have any ideals, beliefs or principles you cannot possibly look at yourself directly. So can you be completely negative, completely quiet, neither thinking nor afraid, and yet be extraordinarily, passionately alive?

That state of mind which is no longer capable of striving is the true religious mind, and in that state of mind you may come upon this thing called truth or reality or bliss or God or beauty or love. This thing cannot be invited. Please understand that very simple fact. It cannot be invited, it cannot be sought after, because the mind is too silly, too small, your emotions are too shoddy, your way of life too confused for that enormity, that immense something, to be invited into your little house, your little corner of living which has been trampled and spat upon. You cannot invite it. To invite it you must know it and you cannot know it. It doesn't matter who says it, the moment he says, 'I know', he does not know. The moment you say you have found it you have not found it. If you say you have experienced it, you have never experienced it. Those are all ways of exploiting another man—your friend or your enemy.

One asks oneself then whether it is possible to come upon this thing without inviting, without waiting, without seeking or exploring—just for it to happen like a cool breeze that comes in when you leave the window open? You cannot invite the wind but you must leave the window open, which doesn't mean that you are in a state of waiting;

that is another form of deception. It doesn't mean you must open yourself to receive; that is another kind of thought.

Haven't you ever asked yourself why it is that human beings lack this thing? They beget children, they have sex, tenderness, a quality of sharing something together in companionship, in friendship, in fellowship, but this thing— why is it they haven't got it? Haven't you ever wondered lazily on occasion when you are walking by yourself in a filthy street or sitting in a bus or are on holiday by the seaside or walking in a wood with a lot of birds, trees, streams and wild animals—hasn't it ever come upon you to ask why it is that man, who has lived for millions and millions of years, has not got this thing, this extraordinary unfading flower? Why is it that you, as a human being, who are so capable, so clever, so cunning, so competitive, who have such marvellous technology, who go to the skies and under the earth and beneath the sea, and invent extraordinary electronic brains—why is it that you haven't got this one thing which matters? I don't know whether you have ever seriously faced this issue of why your heart is empty.

What would your answer be if you put the question to yourself—your direct answer without any equivocation or cunningness? Your answer would be in accordance with your intensity in asking the question and the urgency of it. But you are neither intense nor urgent, and that is because you haven't got energy, energy being passion—and you cannot find any truth without passion—passion with a fury behind it, passion in which there is no hidden want. Passion is a rather frightening thing because if you have passion you don't know where it will take you.

So is fear perhaps the reason why you have not got the energy of that passion to find out for yourself why this quality of love is missing in you, why there is not this flame in your heart? If you have examined your own mind and heart very closely, you will know why you haven't got it. If you are passionate in your discovery to find why you haven't got it, you will know it is there. Through complete negation alone, which is the highest form of passion, that thing which is love, comes into being. Like humility you cannot cultivate love. Humility comes into being when there is a total ending of conceit—then you will never know what it is to be humble. A man who knows what it is to have humility is a vain man. In the same way when you give your mind and your heart, your nerves, your eyes, your whole being to find out the way of life, to see what actually is and go beyond it, and deny completely, totally, the life you live now—in that very denial of the ugly, the brutal, the other comes into being. And you will never know it either. A man who knows that he is silent, who knows that he loves, does not know what love is or what silence is.